# SAVOIA MARCHETTI S.79 IN ACTION

By Roberto Gentilli

Color Illustrations by Don Greer

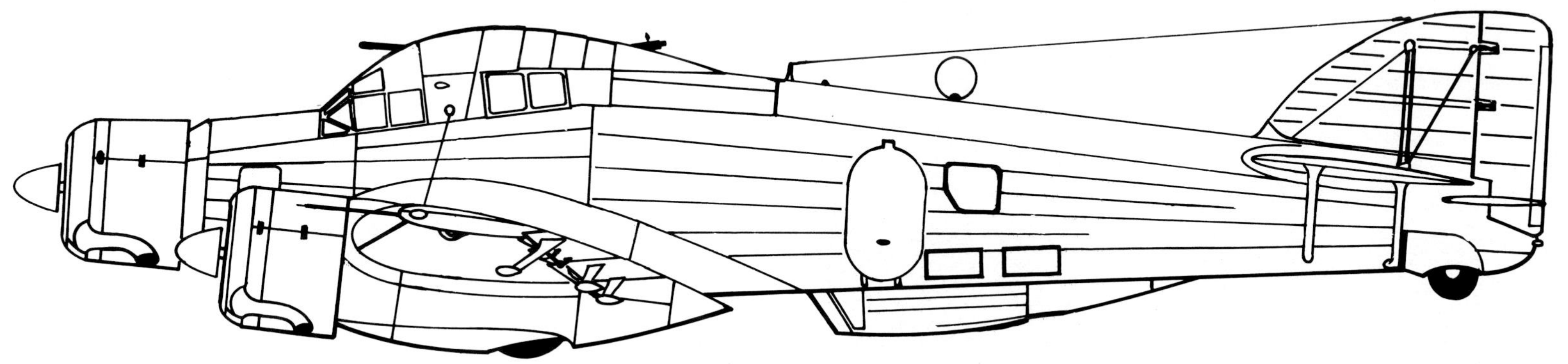

squadron/signal publications

(Cover) The Savoia-Marchetti S.79 torpedo bomber flown by Lieutenant Graziani, 281ª Squadriglia, Rhodes, flies low over the British battleship Barham. Eastern Mediterranean, 13 October 1941.

1115 CROWLEY DRIVE, CARROLLTON, TEXAS 75011-5010



**ISBN 0-89747-173-3**

**If you have any photographs of the aircraft, armor, soldiers or ships of any nation, particularly wartime snapshots, why not share them with us and help make Squadron/Signal's books all the more interesting and complete in the future. Any photograph sent to us will be copied and the original returned. The donor will be fully credited for any photos used. Please indicate if you wish us not to return the photos. Please send them to: Squadron/Signal Publications, Inc., 1115 Crowley Dr., Carrollton, TX 75011-5010.**

## DEDICATION

To Alberto Borgiotti, in remembrance.


# PHOTO CREDITS

## With thanks to:

Aeronautica Militare
Alfa Romeo
Aldo Boileau
Ivana Della Barba
Angelo Emiliani
Cesare Gori
General Giulio Cesare Graziani
Ferenc Kovacs
General Enrico Marescalchi
Giorgio Sacchetti
SIAI Marchetti


**Flying high over Spain, and nearly immune to interception, a formation of S.79s from the 8° Stormo 'Falchi delle Baleari' (Falcons of the Blearics) symbolized Italian air power and political prestige.**

# INTRODUCTION

The Societa Idrovolanti Alta Italia (SIAI), located north of Milan at Sesto Calende, was one of the most successful Italian aircraft manufacturers between World War One and World War Two. The seaplane designs of chief designer Alessandro Marchetti, carrying the proud brand name 'Savoia-Marchetti', had established a reputation for performance and quality construction, and had amassed triumph after triumph in trail-blazing flights across the continents during the years between the wars. One of SIAI most famous aircraft had been the S.55, a twin engined push-pull, twin hulled flying-boat. With Colonel De Pinedo at the controls, the S.55 carried out the first flight across the Atlantic ocean and back in 1927; and the first mass formation flight from Europe to Brazil, in 1931, led by Air Minister Italo Balbo.

In 1933 Balbo with a wing of twenty-four of these seaplanes in its final version, the S.55X, carried out an epoch-making flight from Italy to Chicago and back. This flight, in honor of the Chicago's World Fair, was the high water mark of Italy's policy of gaining national prestige through feats of aviation pursued by Benito Mussolini's fascist dictatorship. Traditionally a manufacturer of seaplanes, SIAI began producing landplanes with the introduction of the S.71, a three engined, high wing, ten passenger transport in 1930. Similar in appearance to the S71, the S.72 first appeared as a commercial transport and in 1935 SIAI delivered six S.72 Bombers to the Central (Nanking) Government Air Force of China. Also in 1934 the S.73, a low wing transport, that used the same thick, one-piece cantilever wing of the S.55, made its appearance.

In 1934 Balbo with a wing of twenty-four of these seaplanes in its final version, the S.55X, carried out an epoch-making flight from Italy to Chicago and back. This flight, in honor of the Chicago's World Fair, was the high water mark of Italy's policy of gaining national prestige through feats of aviation pursued by Benito Mussilini's fascist dictatorship. Traditionally a manufacturer of seaplanes, SIAI began producing landplanes with the introduction of the S.71, a three engined, high wing, ten passenger transport in 1934. Similar in appearance to the S71, the S.72 first appeared as a commercial transport and in 1935 SIAI delivered six S.72 Bombers to the Central (Nanking) Government Air Force of China. Also in 1934 the S.73, a low wing transport, that used the same thick, one-piece cantilever wing of the S.55, made its appearance.

Alessandro Marchetti understood the march of time, and early in 1933 he began designing a fast, eight passenger, three engined low wing monoplane transport, embodying state-of-the-art features. Power was to be provided by three Isotta Fraschini XI R in-line water cooled engines with the intention of entering the new machine in the MacRobertson London to Melbourne air race. Construction was conventional, featuring a welded chrome molybdenum steel tube fuselage framework with a mixed covering of aluminum, plywood and cloth. The wing was a single cantilever unit on three spars, of wooden construction and covering. This type of construction had been brought to a high level of craftsmanship, which required inexpensive raw materials, little capital investment for machine tools and a relatively inexpensive skilled work force. Precisely the conditions then existing in Italian industry.

Under the designation S.79*, Marchetti's design was extremely innovative for its time, featuring a partially retractable main landing gear, the first ever applied to an Italian multi-engined airplane. The design was carefully streamlined and sleek with advanced high lift devices, and long slotted wing flaps automatically connected to Handley Page slots on the leading edge. Externally balanced ailerons drooped to act like flaps, while maintaining their roll control function.

**In 1937 Societa Idrovolanti Alta Italia changed its name to Societa Italiana Aeroplani Idrovolanti SIAI Marchetti. From then on its projects were identified as S.M. Photographs show that the aircraft itself sometimes carried the legend S.79 and sometimes S.M.79. However the S.79 was commonly referred to with only the single letter throughout its career.*

While under construction, the S.79 was readied for the installation of three Fiat A 59 engines (License-built Pratt & Whitney Hornets), however these were replaced by three 610 hp Piaggio P.IX RC 40 nine cylinder radial engines turning SIAI three bladed two pitch propellers. Carrying the registration code I-MAGO (a registration with a double meaning to the Italians: *Imago* meaning image in Latin and *Mago* meaning wizard in Italian) for its first flight, which took place on 8 October 1934 at Cameri airport. It was too late to take part in the MacRobertson International Air Race, but from the first moment test pilot Adriano Bacula and the SIAI technicians knew they had a winner, and one of Europe's most advanced multi-engine aircraft. Its powerplant, however, immediately proved unreliable, and precluded its transferral to the test center at Guidonia-Montecelio, near Rome. Early in 1935 the S.79 P (for Passengers) was fitted with three Alfa Romeo 125 RC 35 580 hp engines, which were Italian developments of the license-built Bristol Pegasus radial engine. Flying for the first time with these new engines on 5 April 1935, maximum speed of 355 km/h (220 mph) at sea level was achieved. On 14 June 1935 a one hour ten minute flight from Milan to Littorio airfield, Rome was made at an average speed of 410 km/H (255 mph).

After testing by *Regia Aeronautica* pilots, it was chosen by *Generale* Giuseppe Valle, the stocky, autocratic, hard driving Chief of Staff, and Mussolini's Under Secretary of the Air Ministry, for a fast inspection tour of Italian East Africa where forces were being massed for the coming invasion of Ethiopia. It was fitted with improved navigational instruments and fuel tanks in the tail of the engine nacelles, and received the military serial M.M.260. On 1 August 1935 it flew to Massawa, Eritrea, via Cairo, Egypt, in twelve hours and returned to Rome four days later. On 24 September 1935 Colonel Biseo established world records for 1,000 km and 2,000 km closed circuits. The SIAI trimotor's remarkable performance impressed the *Regia Aeronautica*, and turned General Valle into a partisan of the S.79.

In late 1935 SIAI felt that a military version of its S.79 was obvious since not only was it the fastest multi-engined airplane in Italy, but it was faster than almost all contemporary fighters. The S.79's performance had made *Regia Aeronautica's* first line bomber, the S.81, just entering production, obsolete. In 1934 *Regia Aeronautica* had issued a competition for a modern medium bomber, requiring a *twin-engined* aircraft capable of carrying 1,200 kilograms of bombs 1,000 kilometers at a top speed of 385 km/h. Since Italian policy was becoming increasingly militaristic, and according to General Douhet's theory of all out aviation warfare a bomber force was considered paramount, the contract would obviously be a big one. All aircraft manufacturers entered the competition with roughly

**(Below) The rugged SIAI S.81 was the standard Italian bomber during the late Thirties. These are Gnome & Rhone powered aircraft from the 54ª Squadriglia, of 15º Stormo taking off from Castel Benito, Libya in 1939.**

similar designs, all with twin fins and rudders, the Fiat B.R.20, the Fiat-CMASA BGA, the Caproni Ca.I35, the Piaggio P.32, the CRDA Cant Z.1011 and the Breda 82. Only the Macchi project, the M.C.91, remained on the drawing board.

SIAI Marchetti attempted to join the design competition by offering a twin engine bomber version of the S.79, powered by either a pair of Gnome & Rhone K.14 Mistral Major radial engines or a pair of Hispano Suiza 12Y in-line engines. However pointing to what they felt would be poor performance, and an unsatisfactory location of bombs and guns in a fuselage that had been designed as an airliner the *Regia Aeronautica* rejected the SIAI proposal out of hand. *Generale* Valle, now an ardent proponent of the Savoia-Marchetti design, felt differently and overuled the *Regia Aeronautica*, placing an order for a batch of twenty-four S.79 bombers. SIAI initially called this new bomber S.79 K, referring to the three K.14 motors that it planned to use. *Regia Aeronautica* however, ordered them replaced with three Alfa Romeo I26 RC 34 engines.

On 6 January 1936 I-MAGO returned to Ethiopia for another well advertised flight by *Generale* Valle. During the course of this flight I-MAGO ran out of fuel and force landed in 'no-mans' land in Ethiopia. After re-supply Valle's tour was successfully completed, returning to Italy ten days later.

I-MAGO was eventually assigned to the 12° Stormo and charged with introducing the new bomber into service. Adapted temporarily as a bomber I-MAGO carried out successful bombing tests at the Furbara bombing range. Retro-fitted as a passenger plane it remained in service as a squadron hack. Eventually receiving three Alpha Romeo 126 RC 34 engines, it was based at Guidonia and used for liaison flights all over Europe, being flown by some of Italy's most important pilots.

## S.79 BOMBER PROTOTYPE

The S.79 bomber prototype, serialled M.M.20663, first flew on 8 July 1936. It was powered by three Alfa Romeo 125 engines. Fuel was provided by six interconnected wing spar mounted tanks housing 2200 liters (582 gallons), and one 150 litter (40 gallon) tank between the center spar and the rear spar outboard of each engine nacelle. A further 410 liter (108 gallon) tank could be mounted in the rear of each engine nacelle.

The fuselage, originally designed for an airliner, with a wide square section, was not-modified, but was grafted with a long streamlined dorsal hump, that was to be the trademark of the S.79 throughout its life, earning it the nickname of *Gobbo* (Hunchback) in the contemporary press, but that the British called it the "damned Hunchback" was only wartime propaganda. Sparviero (Sharrowhawk), the S.79's official name, was never picked up by the airmen who flew it, they simply called it the S.79.

Two pilots sat in a side-by-side position, with the commander in the port seat. The top window panels of the canopy opened for parachute ejection. The frontal part of the dorsal hump housed a fixed Safat 12.7MM gun operated by the pilot, and an aft firing flexible

**(Below) The prototype S.79 I-MAGO as it first appeared in October of 1934 with Piaggio Stella engines and close fitting cowlings with rocker arm fairings. The oil coolers can be seen on top of the cowlings, these were soon replaced with circular oil coolers mounted around the propellers hubs. (SMA)**

**(Above) The S.79 prototype, now powered by a trio of Alfa Romeo 125 engines, warms up before take-off. The oil coolers can be seen mounted inside the cowlings behind the propellers. The elaborate fasces emblem on the central cowling carries the inscription A/XIII (thirteenth year of fascist rule). (SMA)**

**(Below) The Alfa 125 powered I-MAGO during Generale Valle's second inspection tour of Ethiopia in January of 1936. Aircraft in the background are Fiat C.R.20 fighters and Caproni Ca.101 bombers. Shadows indicate that its early morning with all airmen, even so near the Equator, wearing overcoats.**

**(Above) The final configuration of the S.79 prototype with Alfa Romeo 126 motors. The inscription on the fin carries the speed and payload records set on 23 September 1935. Colors were Ivory White and Blue. The Black I for Italy, repeated on the horzontal tail surfaces, was standard practice at the time.**

**(Above) The first S.79, delivered in October of 1936, initially had a glazed center section in the hump.**

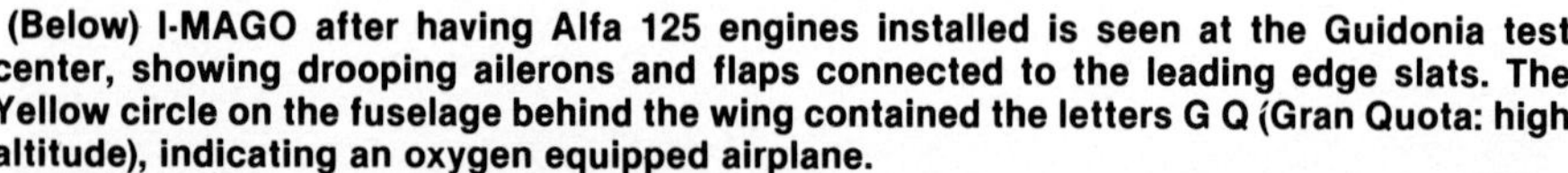

**(Below) I-MAGO after having Alfa 125 engines installed is seen at the Guidonia test center, showing drooping ailerons and flaps connected to the leading edge slats. The Yellow circle on the fuselage behind the wing contained the letters G Q (Gran Quota: high altitude), indicating an oxygen equipped airplane.**

**(Below) The same airplane after being modified with a hump similar to the one found on the initial S.79 production series. The officers of Grottaglie training field are welcoming Generale Valle during an inspection tour in 1937. Fasces emblems are on each engine cowling but not on wings. That the rudder is not vertically striped in the Green-White-Red Italian national colors is unusual.**

mounted 12.7MM machine gun for rear protection. Behind the pilots were the positions of the flight engineer on the port side and the radio operator on the starboard side. The central part of the fuselage was turned into a bomb bay, offset to starboard in order to provide space for a catwalk connecting fore and aft. Bomb loads included two 500 kg (1,102 lb) bombs or five 250 kg (551 lb) bombs or twelve 100 kg (220 lb) bombs or twelve dispensers for 676 2 kg (4.4 lb) fragmentation bombs. All bombs were stored vertically (the heavier ones pointing downward).

The bomb aimer sat in a ventral gondola which had a frontal clear plastic panel protected by a vertically sliding door. When he operated the Jozza bombsight, controlling the rudder with a steering wheel and dropping the bombs with a keyboard known as "the Typewriter" his legs protruded from the tub into two light alloy bins. The tail of this gondola provided a position for an additional 12.7MM Breda Safat machine gun. A single 7.7MM Lewis gun was mounted on a crossbar in the fuselage above the gondola allowing it to be fired from either port or starboard beam hatches installed in the fuselage sides. Crew entry was via a downward hinged doorway with a built-in ladder.

The S.79 bomber prototype, painted Ivory White and trimmed in Blue, was tested at Guidonia and was used extensively by *Generale* Valle as his personal aircraft.

# Developments

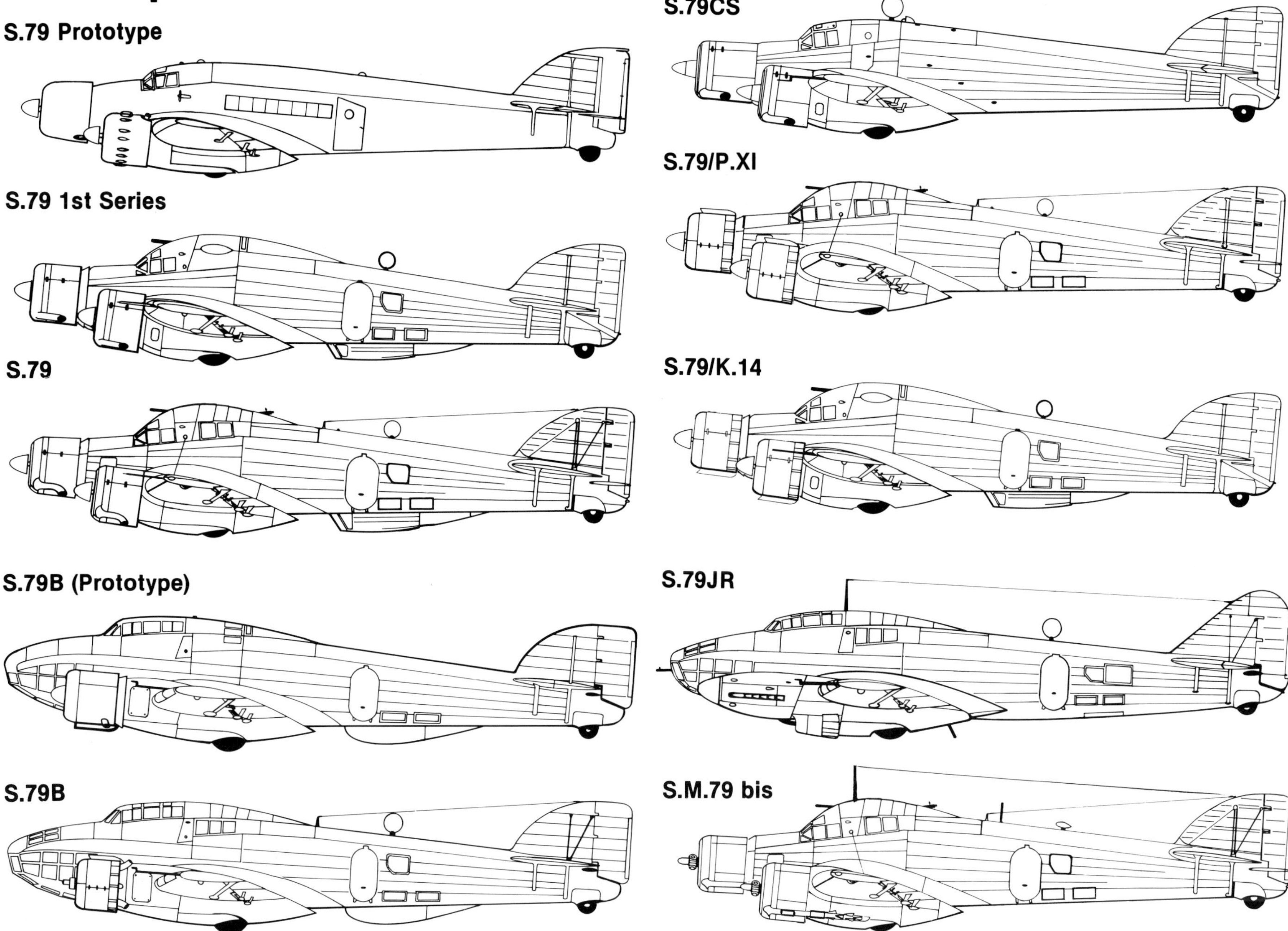

# EARLY PRODUCTION

The first batch or 'series' of twenty-four SIAI S.79 aircraft (serialed M.M.20663 to 20686) was recognizable by the long hump extending along the spine from the cockpit to a point corresponding to the entry door. Teardrop shaped lateral fairings, with sliding panels were mounted just behind the cockpit on both sides of the fuselage. The set of windows which appeared in the hump of the prototype had been eliminated. These twenty-four pre-series aircraft were delivered to the 12° *Stormo* at Guidonia during the Winter of 1936-37, being immediately followed by a further twenty-four (M.M.21157 to M.M.21180). Lateral armament in the first batches of airplanes was a single drum fed .303 Lewis gun of World War One vintage mounted on a sliding rail so as to be able to fire from either the starboard or port window. Later aircraft carried single hand held Safat 7.7MM machine guns mounted in the port and starboard windows, although S.79s prior to the outbreak of the war were usually delivered without the side mounted machine guns. Except the prototype and a few aircraft from the first batch that used the Alfa I25 engine, all production S.79 bombers were equipped with three 750 hp Alfa Romeo I26 RC 34 engines.

The definitive production S.79 had a redesigned shortened dorsal hump. A pair of windows were added to each side of the hump for use by the Wireless Operator and Flight Engineer. In this form the S.79 was to remain in large scale production for almost seven years, without major modification.

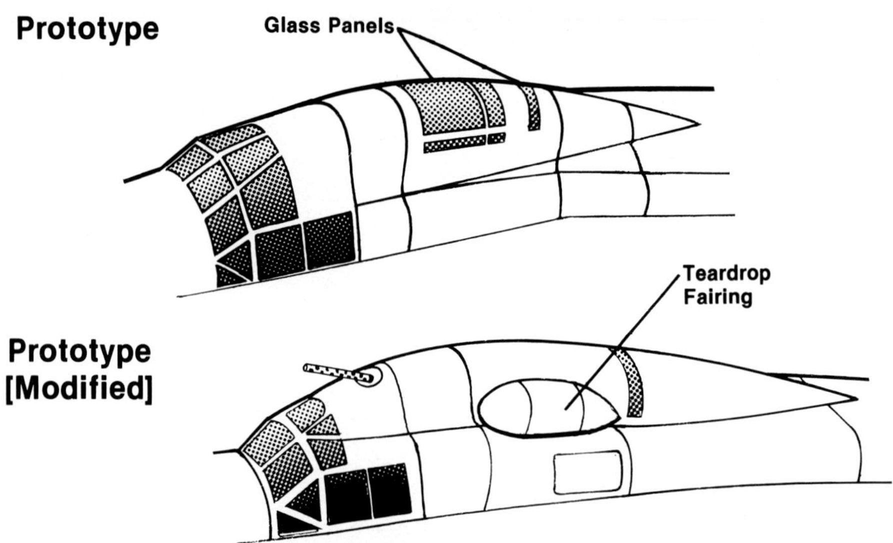


(Below) The first production S.79 bomber (M.M.20663) was initially delivered with a glazed nose section in the top of the hump, however, these were replaced by a pair of teardrop fairings.

(Above and Below) Front and rear view of the Bomber prototype at Guidonia. Powerplants are three Alfa Romeo 125s.

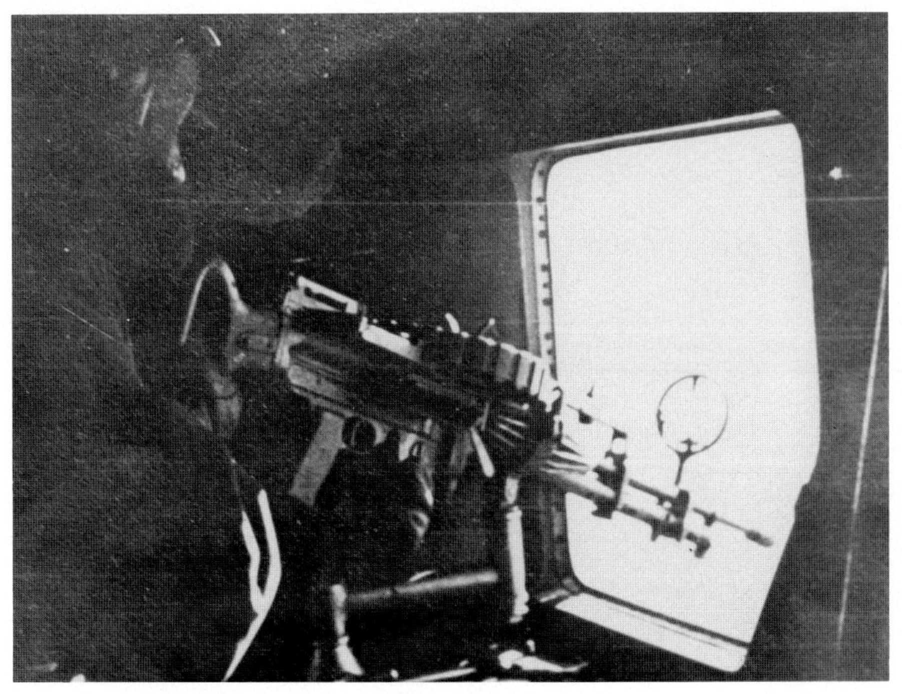

(Above) Early S.79s were armed at the mid-fuselage position with a WWI drum fed Lewis gun mounted on a crossbar allowing it to slide from port to starboard.

(Above Right) The wireless compartment in an S.79 was equipped with an R.A.350 transmitter and an A.R.8 receiver.

## Mid-Mounted 303 Lewis Gun

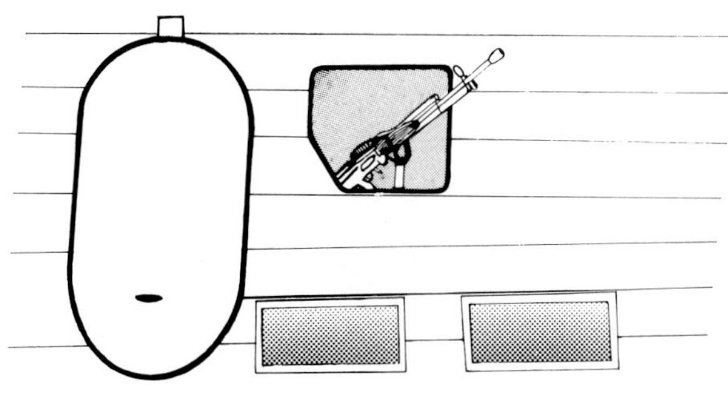

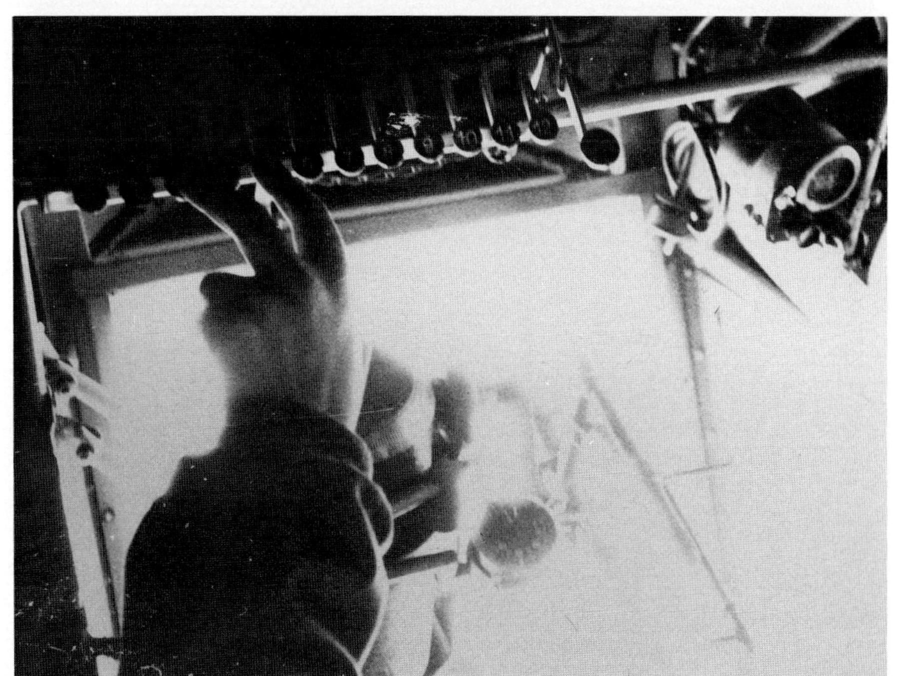

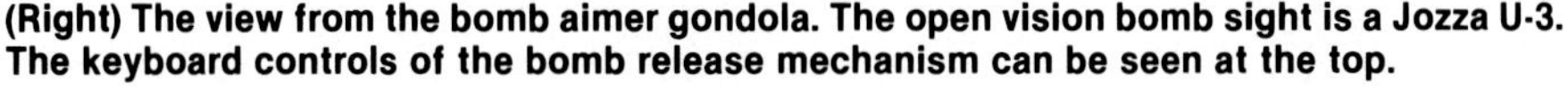

(Right) The view from the bomb aimer gondola. The open vision bomb sight is a Jozza U-3. The keyboard controls of the bomb release mechanism can be seen at the top.

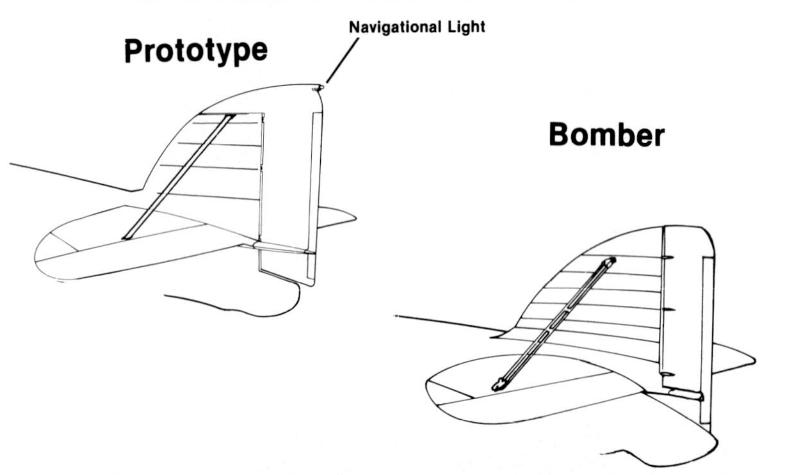

(Above) This early production S.79 with the teardrop fairing just behind the cockpit is seen during tests with the 12° Stormo and is totally devoid of markings. The electrical generator usually placed below the cockpit has been mounted across the starboard window.(SMA)

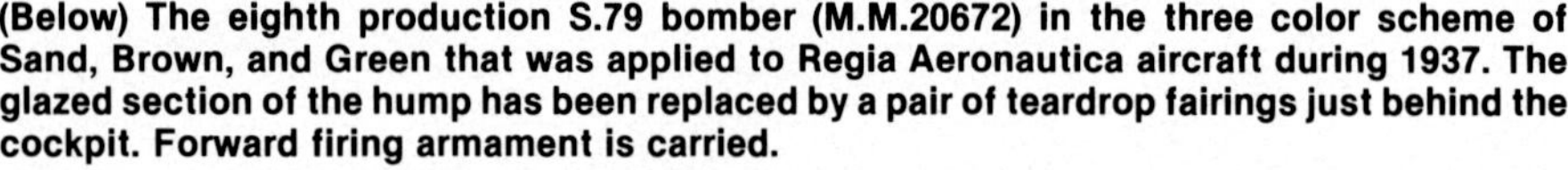

(Below) The eighth production S.79 bomber (M.M.20672) in the three color scheme of Sand, Brown, and Green that was applied to Regia Aeronautica aircraft during 1937. The glazed section of the hump has been replaced by a pair of teardrop fairings just behind the cockpit. Forward firing armament is carried.

# S.79

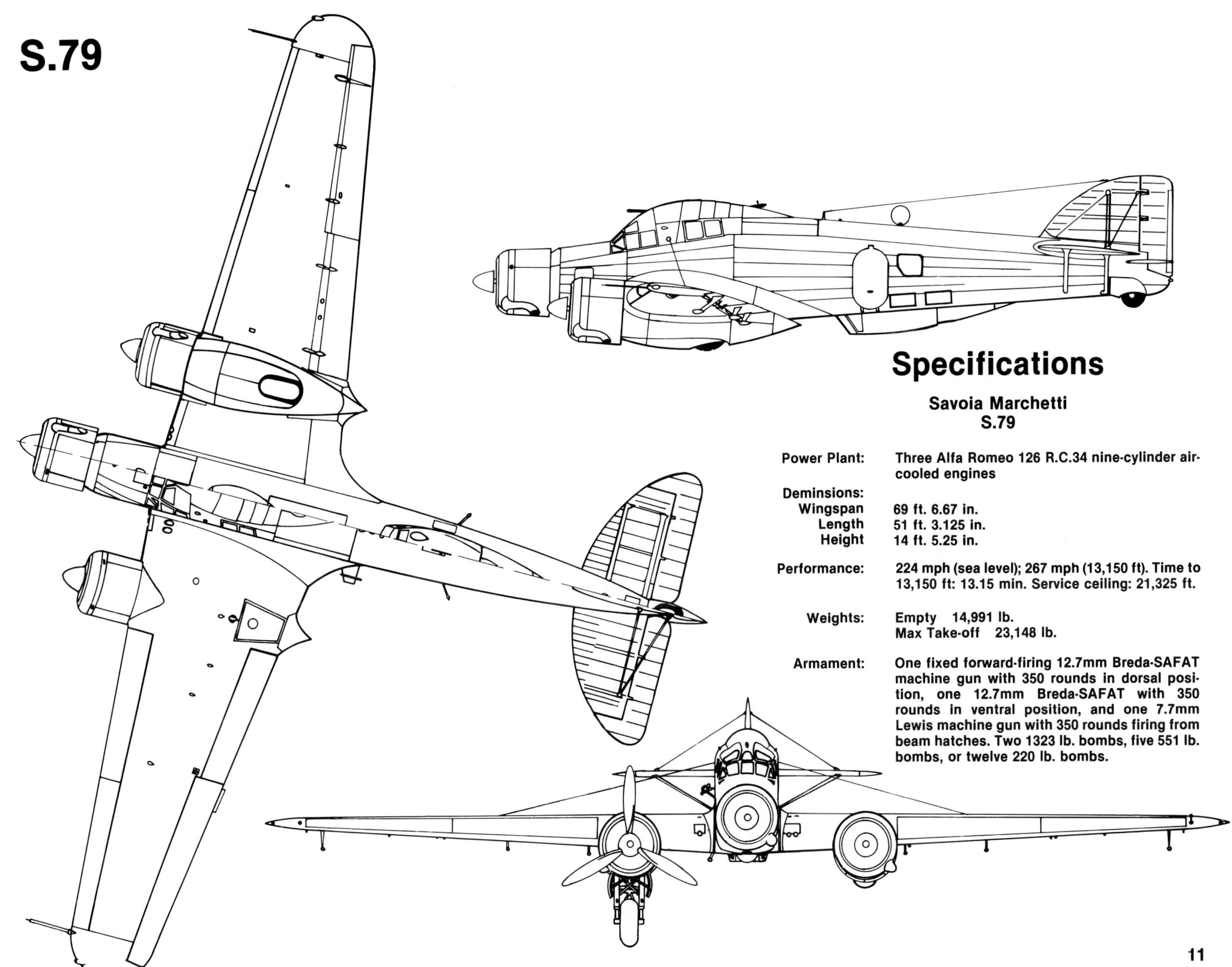

## Specifications

**Savoia Marchetti**
**S.79**

**Power Plant:** Three Alfa Romeo 126 R.C.34 nine-cylinder air-cooled engines

**Deminsions:**
- Wingspan: 69 ft. 6.67 in.
- Length: 51 ft. 3.125 in.
- Height: 14 ft. 5.25 in.

**Performance:** 224 mph (sea level); 267 mph (13,150 ft). Time to 13,150 ft: 13.15 min. Service ceiling: 21,325 ft.

**Weights:** Empty 14,991 lb.
Max Take-off 23,148 lb.

**Armament:** One fixed forward-firing 12.7mm Breda-SAFAT machine gun with 350 rounds in dorsal position, one 12.7mm Breda-SAFAT with 350 rounds in ventral position, and one 7.7mm Lewis machine gun with 350 rounds firing from beam hatches. Two 1323 lb. bombs, five 551 lb. bombs, or twelve 220 lb. bombs.

# Service Introduction

*Regia Aeronautica* felt that pilots transitioning from the lumbering 160 km/h (100 mph) biplanes then in service, to the 420 km/h (260 mph) S.79, that was faster than most contemporary fighters, would experience difficulty in converting to the high performance bomber. To facilitate aircrew transitioning to the S.79 12° *Stormo Bombardamento Terrestre* was formed at Guidonia where it took delivery of the twenty-four S.79 pre-series (serialed from M.M.20663 to M.M.20686) between October of 1936 and January of 1937. The 12° *Stormo* was formed with the most experienced pilots, mostly drawn from veterans of the Balbo cruises and fighter units. The 12° Stormo was made up of two *Gruppi* (Groups) 41 and 42, of which only the former was operational at Guidonia.

The S.79 found itself in the paradoxical situation of being an admired and successful airplane, but an unwanted bomber. *Regia Aeronautica* Technical Branch was opposed to its trimotor configuration, its primitive defensive armament with hand-held guns in open positions, the location of the bomb aimer in a ventral 'tub' from which the bombardier legs protruded. But most of all, criticism was levelled at the small bomb-bay, located in what was to all intents and purposes, an airliner fuselage, with bombs hanging vertically and therefore having an erratical dropping pattern. However the main reason for the S.79's success was due the failure of its competitors. Of all the aircraft presented for the 1934 bomber competition, only the Fiat B.R.20, which began to enter squadron service in 1937, and would suffer a long period of teething troubles, would in any way be considered successful. The Piaggio P.32, according to a few pilots was 'a misunderstood Italian B-25 Mitchell', but according to most it was a 'flying coffin'. The mixed construction Caproni Ca.l35 had four different types of engines installed without attaining an acceptable level of efficiency.

Early in 1937 *Regia Aeronautica* was increasing its air units according to a rearmament plan which would be continually rewritten until it became the 1939 'Plan R' calling for some 3,000 first-line aircraft. The staff Offices envisioned thirty-four bomber *Squadriglie* of B.R.20s, thirty-four *Squadriglie* of Caproni 135s, and twenty-four *Squadriglie* of Piaggio P.32s*. The ambitious planners of the Staff Offices were unaware that Valle had already reduced production orders for the Ca.135 and the P.32 to only thirty-two machines each. While the great production scheme of the SIAI S.81 Pipistrello was successfully implemented, the same license building pattern would be applied to the S.79, which had a nearly identical construction, simple wooden wings and welded tube fuselage.

As dissatisfaction with the progress being made with the various twin engine bomber designs increased, added importance was placed on the S.79. Even before the first of the twenty-four pre-series was completed SIAI received an order for an additional eighty-two aircraft, and Aeronautica Macchi received an order for twenty-four license built S.79s, with license production later being joined by Reggiane and Aeronautica Umbra S.A. (AUSA) at Foligno, in Central Italy. By the spring of 1937 orders had been placed for 202 S.79s. While a single Ca.135 had yet to be delivered to the *Regia Aeronautica*, the S.79 was amassing combat triumphs in the Spanish Civil War, and by the fall of 1937 *Regia Aeronautica* plans had been changed to thirty-four *Squadriglie* of B.R.20s, and twenty of Ca.135s (powered by an engine that didn't yet exist), and fifty *Squadriglie* of S.79s.

Throughout 1937 the number of S.79s in service grew very slowly, even though Macchi and Reggiane joined with license production, followed by AUSA in 1939. The 8° *Stormo* from Bologna was the second unit to receive the S.79, followed by the 9° *Stormo* of Ciampino, Rome. Both of these units had previously flown the S.81. The dispatch of S.79s to Spain somewhat slowed down *Regia Aeronautica's* build-up of the new bomber, but one by one the S.81 *stormi* converted to the S.79, and new units were formed on the new bomber. During the summer of 1938, with Europe seemingly on the edge of war, *Regia Aeronautica* could field only some 150 S.79s. A year later just over 300 S.79s were on strength. On 10 June 1940, when Italy declared war on France and Great Britain, following the Nazi invasion of France, the S.79 equipped fourteen *stormi* and one independent *gruppo* with a total strength of 612 S.79s.

Deployment of S.79 units were as follows:

**2nd Air Force - Sicily**
*Stormi* 11° 30° 34° 36° 41°

**3rd Air Force - Central Italy**
*Stormi* 9° 12° 46°

**Air Force of Sardinia**
*Stormi* 8° 32°

**Air Force of Lybia**
*Stormi* 10° 14° (partially equipped) 15° 33°

**Air Force of East Africa**
*44°* Gruppo

*Stormo = two *Gruppi*
*Gruppo* = two *Squadriglie*
*Squadriglia* = six aircraft

**(Above) Newly delivered S.79s of the 52ª Squadriglia, 8° Stormo, low over the Appennine hills near Bologna during 1937. The first two bombers carry the squadron number, but no aircraft number as yet. The national insignia of three fasces on a White circle, adopted in 1936, has not been painted on the wings.**

It was an impressive force, conceived for a *lightning war* which would last only a few weeks and would be decided by these fast uninterceptable bombers. Only the 1st Air Force in Northern Italy had no S.79s, being equipped with the B.R.20 at its western bases (around Fiat's hometown of Turin), and the Cant Z. 1007.

This bomber force, internationally exalted by Italian propaganda, was mauled in daylight encounters with modern British monoplane fighters. The proud bomber *Stormi* were literally chewed up in courageous but ineffective massed daylight attacks on the British Fleet, against the fortress island of Malta, and over the Western Desert. The S.79, obviously outclassed by British aircraft, seemed destined to second-line duties such as convoy protection, strategic reconnaissance and as a high-speed VIP transport.

The reluctant bomber, however, would find itself a new role, that of torpedo bomber, which would breath new operational life into the design and bring it additional acclaim. From the first experimental attacks during the Summer of 1940 to the final operations of Mussolini's *Aeronautica Nazionale Republicana* in early 1945, a small group of overworked aircrew and S.79s supplied one of the most effective elements of Italy's contribution to the Axis air war effort.

**(Above) An S.79 carrying the civil registration (I-SVSF or I-SVSI) from the Scuola Volo Senza Visibilita (Blind flying School) at Littoria. This machine carries Green-White-Red stripes around the wings and fuselage over the standard Sand-Brown-Green camouflage and a Black I on the rudder. No armament is carried. (Emiliani)**

**(Below) 13-7 of the 26 Gruppo, 9º Stormo. This unit was created on 26 February 1934 at Ciampino, Rome and in 1936 received SIAI S.81. On 15 October 1937 it was moved to Viterbo, Central Italy, receiving the S.79. (Emiliani)**

**(Below) S.79s of 193ª Squadriglia, 30º Stormo carrying the early segmented scheme. The second aircraft does not have the regulation Green, White, and Red rudder.**

(Left) S.79 from 59ª Squadriglia preparing to land at Ferrara. No frontal or lateral armament is carried. The effect of stress on the fuselage fabric is clearly visible. The under surfaces of these aircraft are painted Silver.

(Above) A close formation of S.79s belonging to the 59ª Squadriglia of 11° Stormo from Ferrara. The wing insignia is very noticeable on the Green with Sand Brown mottle camouflage introduced in 1938.

(Above) The Alfa Romeo 126 RC 34 engine of the S.79.

(Left) Mass parades of aircraft multiplied in the late Thirties, propagandizing the air might of Mussolini's Fascist government. S.79s from 46ª Squadriglia, 33º Stormo from Capodichino, Naples, are lined up with Fiat C.R.32 fighters. Propellers are placed according to regulations, with one blade pointing upwards.

(Above) A forced landing for an S.79 of 67ª Squadriglia, 34° Gruppo, 11° Stormo in 1938. The camouflage of Brown and Green mottle over Sand appears somewhat shiny. No wing insignias are carried.

(Above) A spectacular crash of 68-5 from 11° Stormo on 17 November 1939, but fortunately with no casualties. The individual aircraft number was repeated in White in front of the cockpit and on the wing leading edges.

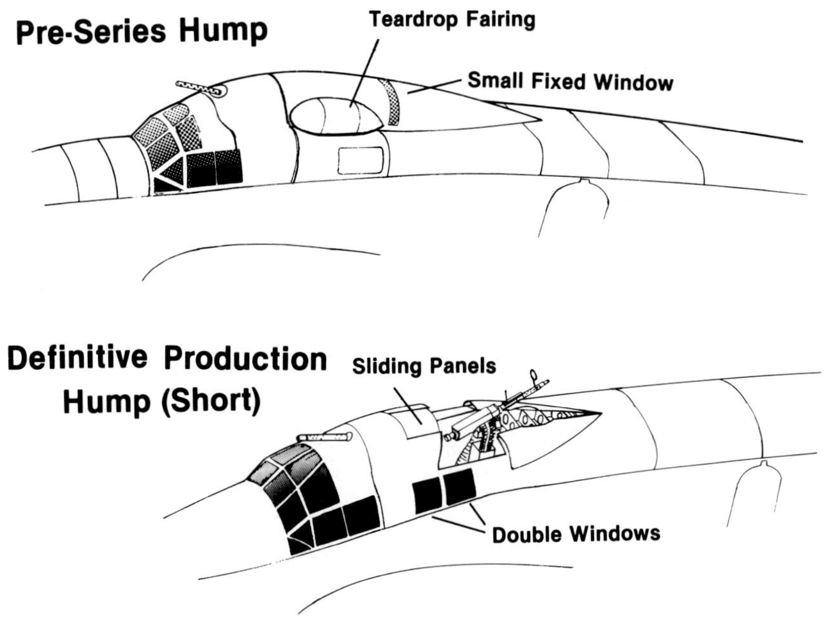

(Right) A formation of 11° Stormo aircraft in flight above the plains of the Po valley. The open dorsal position made the taking of spectacular photos very easy. Although war is obviously nearing, all aircraft are devoid of frontal and side armament because of a scarcity of machine guns.

# Exhaust System

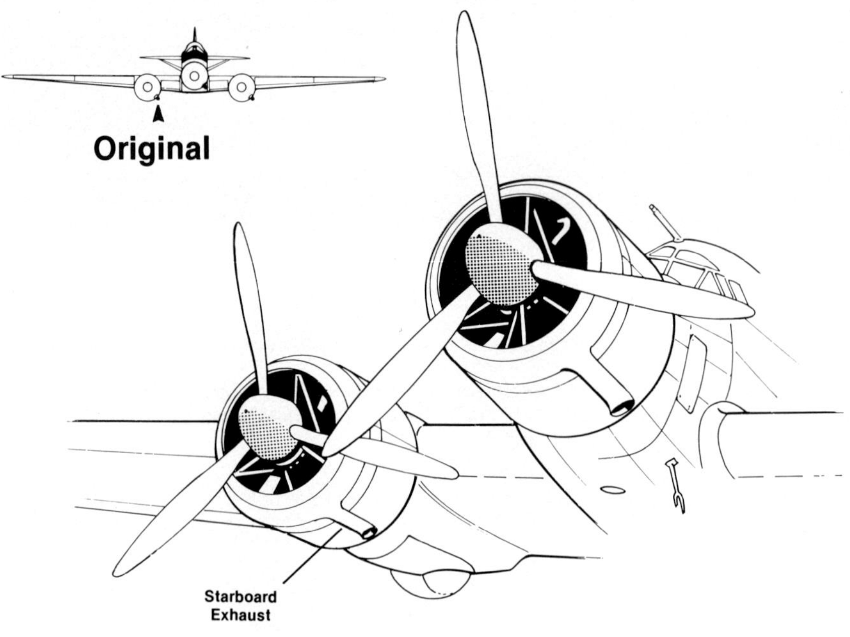


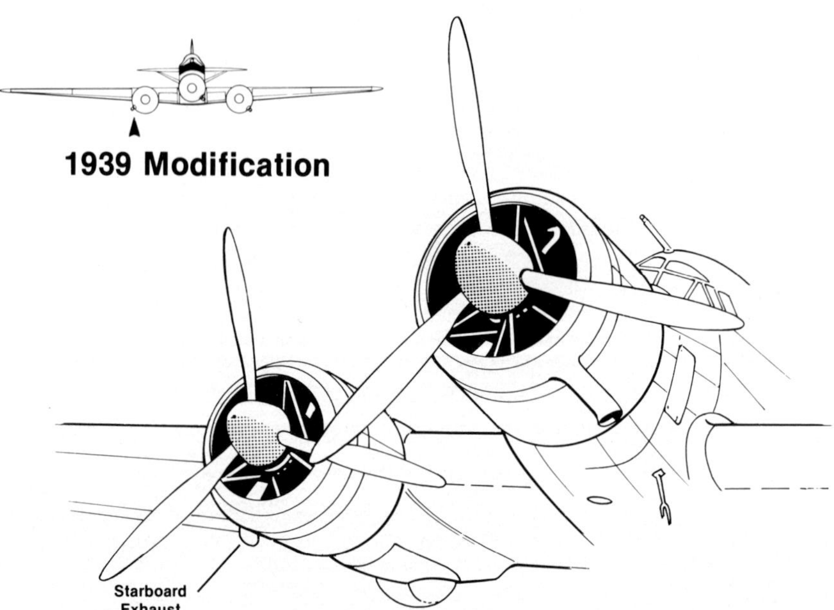

**(Above) 68-5 of 11° Stormo upside down in the rich farmland near Ferrara. This machine was eventually repaired and returned duty. The robust construction of the S.79 was a big asset under combat conditions.**

**(Below) This S.79 carries a regular mottled color scheme. In testing the S.79 at night it was found that the hot glowing exhaust pipe of the starboard engine blinded the bomb aimer. By 1939 most S.79s had the starboard exhaust moved to the outside of the engine.**

# S.79 RACERS

During the Spring of 1937 SIAI completed five S.79 airframes (constructor's numbers 51, 52, 53, 54 and 55), as special long range racers for the *Ministero dell'Aeronautica* under the designation S.79 CS (CS = *Corsa)* racer. They were specially modified to take part in the air race from New York to Paris, organized by the *Aero Club de France* to celebrate the tenth anniversary of Charles Lindbergh's flight. The five S.79 CS received serials M.M.355 to M.M.359. The CS was built with a clean smooth fuselage, no gondola or dorsal hump, which contained long range fuel tanks. Neither door nor window marred the smoothness of the fuselage, entry for the crew being through a hatch behind the canopy. Particular attention was taken with detailing and finish.

Specially tuned Alfa Romeo 126 engines were fitted with French Ratier propellers. The carefully finished racers were painted in Glossy Red (Italy's car and aircraft racing color) with White and Green trim. Elite pilots of the 12 ° *Stormo* to whom the racers were assigned christened them *Sorci Verdi* (Green Mice, Italian slang for 'incredible things').

The Lindbergh Trophy, for which *Regia Aeronautica* had spared no effort, had to be cancelled, but was replaced by a race from Istres, in Southern France, to Damascus, Syria, and back to Paris, with a non-stop stretch corresponding to the flight across the Atlantic. The five trimotors got special civil registrations derived from the initial letters of their respective pilot's surnames: I-BIMU, I-TOMO, I-CUPA, I-FILU and I-LICA. Particularly remarkable was the crew of I-BIMU, with Italy's number one pilot Attilio Biseo and Bruno Mussolini, the son of the dictator.

The five S.79's were joined by two Caproni Ca.405 *Procellaria*, a development of the Piaggio P.32, and two Fiat B.R.20s entered by Fiat to prove their worth against the SIAI Marchetti rival. When one of the Ca.405s defaulted, a sixth S.79 (serialled M.M.21117), was rushed to take its place. Carrying the registration I-ROTR, it retained its military protuberances. French competitors in the Istres-Damascus-Paris event included prototypes from Bloch, Farman, Breguet and Caudron, plus a British DH-88 Comet.

The race was held on 20 August 1937 and was dominated by the Italian S.79 CS. Only I-LICA, damaged on take off from Damascus airfield, had to retire, while all the others flew across the Mediterranean, landing in Paris on 21 August to score a 1,2,3,6, and 8 place victory for the SIAI trimotor. Fascist propaganda over the 'Green Mice' was long and loud, further establishing the Savoia Marchetti S.79 as Italy's foremost aircraft.

Three S.79 CSs were converted to S.79 Ts (Trans-Atlantic) and prepared for a South Atlantic crossing, on a route where scheduled airline service was being planned. M.M.359 I-BIMU became I-BISE, M.M.358 I-CUPA became I-MONI, and M.M.356 I-FILU became I-BRUN indicating each airplane's commander: Biseo with Paradisi, Nino Moscatelli with Gori Castellani and Bruno Mussolini with Mancinelli. After detailed preparation, the three S.79 Ts took off on 24 January 1938 for the record flight to Rio de Janeiro, Brazil, via Dakar, Senegal, the route of many previous pioneering ocean flights.

The three 'Green Mice' flew almost 10,000 km at an average speed of 400 km/h (248 mph), landing in Rio on the evening of 25 January, with one S.79 being slowed down by propeller trouble. This flight was possibly the final act of the Golden Age of Aviation prior to the outbreak of the Second World War. This last pioneering flight was further emphasized in the Italian media because of the presence of Bruno Mussolini. The three aircraft were presented to the Brazilian Air Service, which serialled them K.420, 421 and 422. In 1938 they were joined by a standard S.79 bomber sent to Brazil to stimulate an order for Italian warplanes that did not materialize. These aircraft had limited activity due to a lack of spares and support. They were were struck off Brazillian charge in 1943/44.

**(Above) The S.79 CS racer as it first appeared, still carrying SIAI PWO 2 propellers. The CS had a very sleek finish, with faired tail bracing cables. The object on the spine of the fuselage was an air vent for the fuselage mounted fuel tanks.**

**(Below) The S.79 CS was fitted with Ratier propellers. A fascist symbol has been added to the central cowling which is burnished natural Metal. The crew entry door can be seen in the open position behind the cockpit glass. (SMA)**

(Above) The Italian competitors in the Istres-Damascus-Paris race at the Guidonia test air base. I-8 and I-10 are two of the Fiat B.R.20s, which Fiat hoped would demonstrate its superiority over the rival S.79. (SMA)

(Above) I-LICA flown by Lippi and Castellani carrying the racing number I-7 after its aborted take-off from Damascus airfield.

(Below) The standard S.79 bomber I-ROTR, which placed eighth in the race, arrives at Rome's Aeroporto del Littorio (now Urbe Airport) to a triumphant welcome. In the background can be seen the airport's typical two storied hangars.

(Above) Benito Mussolini, with Generale Valle behind him, welcomes the 'Green mice' pilots at the Aeroporto del Littorio. Standing fourth from right is Mussolini's own son, nineteen year old Bruno Mussolini, who died in 1941 testing a Piaggio P.108 bomber.

## Tail Cables

Initial:
Twin Cables

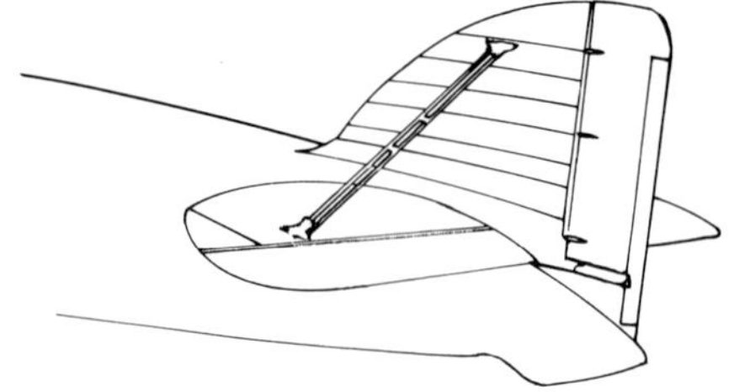

Production:
Twin Cables
plus
Additional Cable

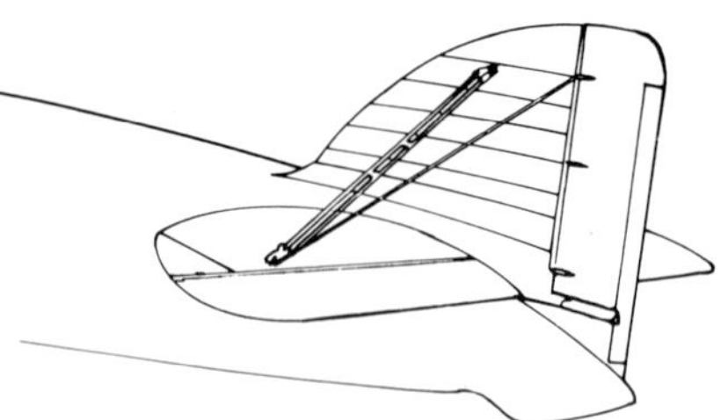

(Above) S.79 racer I-MONI (formerly I-CUPA), carrying the race number I-11 in honor of the Istres-Damascus-Paris race, at Guidonia during preparation for the Atlantic flight. From this angle the S.79's airliner heritage is apparent. (SMA)

(Below) SIAI test pilots Adriano Bacula (second from left) and De Ambrosis (fourth from left) in front of S.79 CS I-TOMO on 30 November 1937, after having raced it for a speed-with-payload record against the military S.79/P.XI. (SMA)

(Above) This 'Green mice' S.79 I-BISE was formerly I-5 I-BIMU. Markings are mixed, with civil registration and I for Italy on the rudder, and also the military State Shield on the White rudder stripe. The aircraft in the background is a SIAI S.73 airliner. (SMA)

(Below) S.79 205-1 of the 41° Gruppo, 12° Stormo, with the 'Green mice' insignia of the S.79 Racers, assigned to that unit in September of 1937. Both empty and loaded weights of the aircraft are marked on the rudder. Early in the war, in just over a one year period, this unit operated the S.79, the S.M.82, the Cant Z.1007s bis, the S.M.84 and again the S.79. (Rovere)

# S.79B TWIN ENGINE BOMBER

A twin engined version of the S.79, under the designation S.79 B *(Bimotor)*, was designed in 1935 in order to comply with *Regia Aeronautica* requirements expressed in the bomber competition of 1934. Rejected by the *Ministero dell'Aeronautica*, development of the Bimotor was continued as a company funded project with an eye toward possible export sales.

Using airframe c/n 9, a glazed nose section containing a bomb aiming station was grafted onto a standard fuselage with provisions being made for two 12.7 MM Breda-SAFAT machine guns on flexible mounts, one beneath sliding panels at the rear of the dorsal hump and one in the tail of the ventral gondola which was retained as a defensive position The outboard engine mountings were lengthened in order to maintain the center of gravity (COG). The dorsal hump was extended aft with the cockpit being raised, moved forward, and narrowed, providing much better aerodynamics. The co-pilot was now seated behind the pilot in a tandem arrangement. The rudder area was enlarged to ensure lateral control.

First flying on 8 August 1936, power was provided by a pair of 950 hp Gnome & Rhone K.14 Mistral Major fourteen cylinder two row radial engines. Maximum speed was 420 km/h (261 mph) and range with a 1250 kg (2756 lb) bomb load was 1600 km (994 miles).

During the late Summer of 1936 the S.79 B, carrying the registration I-AYRE, was shipped to Argentina with a SIAI mission, to take part in a competition to provide the Argentine Air Force with a new bomber. The S.79 B was test flown against the German Junkers Ju 86 and the American Martin 139W. A final decision in favor of the American bomber came in the Spring of 1937, and I-AYRE was shipped back to Italy.

The second S.79 was equipped with two Fiat A 80 motors, the 1000 hp units that equipped the B.R.20. First flying in November 1936, this aircraft had a modified hump with lateral teardrop fairings. It was prepared for Iraq, which had also placed an order for Italian A 80-equipped Breda 65 attack monoplanes.

Carrying the serial number 100 in Arabic numerals, c/n 11 was delivered in July of 1937, followed by four more, (101-104) in early 1938. Aircraft 101-104 had additional glazed panels above the nose section, humps like those on the standard trimotor, big double windows, and no teardrop fairings. S.79 B 100 was damaged during the Summer of 1937 and remained in Italy for repairs for some two years, returning to Iraq only in 1939. The Royal Iraqi Air Force quickly mastered the sophisticated bomber, and when hostilities erupted between the Iraqi armed forces and the British in May of 1941, the S.79 B flew missions, only to be put quickly out of action by the RAF. A single survivor was employed as a transport in the Middle East for some years.

The most important export customer of the S.79 was *Fortelor Aeriene Regal ale Romania* (Royal Air Forces of Romania) usually shortened to *FARR*, which ordered twenty-four S.79 Bs powered by a pair of 900 hp Romanian-built IAR K.14 engines, a license built version of the Gnome-Rhone 14K Mistral Major. With only minor changes, such as the installation of a 7.92 MM machine gun in the nose position, these were delivered from the Spring of 1938 to the Spring of 1939. One ferry flight ending in tragedy, with the death of test pilot Bacula and flight engineer Merizzi. The S.79Bs were in service with *FARR* at the outbreak of the war in the East, and fought successfully during operations against Russia in 1941.

## S.79 JR

In 1939 Romania requested SIAI to modify the S.79 B to accept the 1220 hp German Junkers Jumo 211 Da in-line water cooled engine, with plans for the license production by the *Industria Aeronautica Romana* (IAR) company of Brasov, Romania. The first Italian S.79 JR (Junkers-Romania) flew in March of 1941, with a batch of eight aircraft being delivered during the course of the year. Maximum speed was 444 km/h (276 mph) and range with maximum bomb load was 1352 km (840 miles). Sometimes designated J.R.S. 79B, this bomber had a completely redesigned and enlarged fin and rudder, and finally did away with the ventral gondola, a rounded fairing streamlining the bottom of the fuselage, which had provisions for a machine gun to be fired through a hatch. IAR produced aircraft carried an additional pair of large windows in the rear fuselage. Romanian production during 1941 was intensive, with wartime reports putting Romanian construction at over a hundred machines, equipping three squadrons of *Grupul 2* which remained operational into 1944. In 1948 a Romanian S.79 was flown to Italy by a Romanian pilot escaping the communist regime. It was turned over to the Experimental Unit at Guidonia airfield, being scrapped in 1950.

**(Below) The S.79 B prototype carrying a dorsal hump similar to the one on M.M.20663, the bomber prototype, and an enlarged rudder. This airplane was registered I-AYRE and remained in Argentina for almost a year.**

**(Above) The S.79B competed against the Martin 139W and the Junkers Ju 86, losing to the American Martin bomber. After its return from Argentina I-AYRE was demonstrated around Europe hoping to capture export contracts.**

**(Below) S.79 Bs of the Royal Iraqi Air Force, powered by Fiat A 80 motors. Iraqi aviators had few problems in adapting to this relatively sophisticated but reliable warplane.**

**(Below) A Romanian S.79 B at Guidonia airfield prior to delivery. The extensively glazed nose section provided an excellent bombardier position. In the hangar in the background is a Romeo Ro.51 fixed landing gear monoplane fighter.**

**(Above) An S.79 B sold to Romania while under test at Guidonia. The airplane carries the standard Italian Sand-Brown-Green segmented 1937-style camouflage. The Romanian national colors of Blue, Red and Yellow appear to be painted in the wrong color order.**

**(Above Right) View from the glazed nose of a Romanian S.79 B during early operations against the Soviet Union, summer 1941. The machine gun is a drum fed Belgian manufactured 7.9MM FN.**

**(Below Right) A Romanian-built J.R.S.79 B on a snow covered airfield during operations late in the war. (Bundesarchiv)**

**(Below) The first SIAI-built S.79 JR with Jumo 211 Da inline engines during test flights at Cameri in 1941. The airplane is carrying temporary Italian markings, including Yellow engine cowls as prescribed for Italian aircraft in 1941.**

# S.79JR

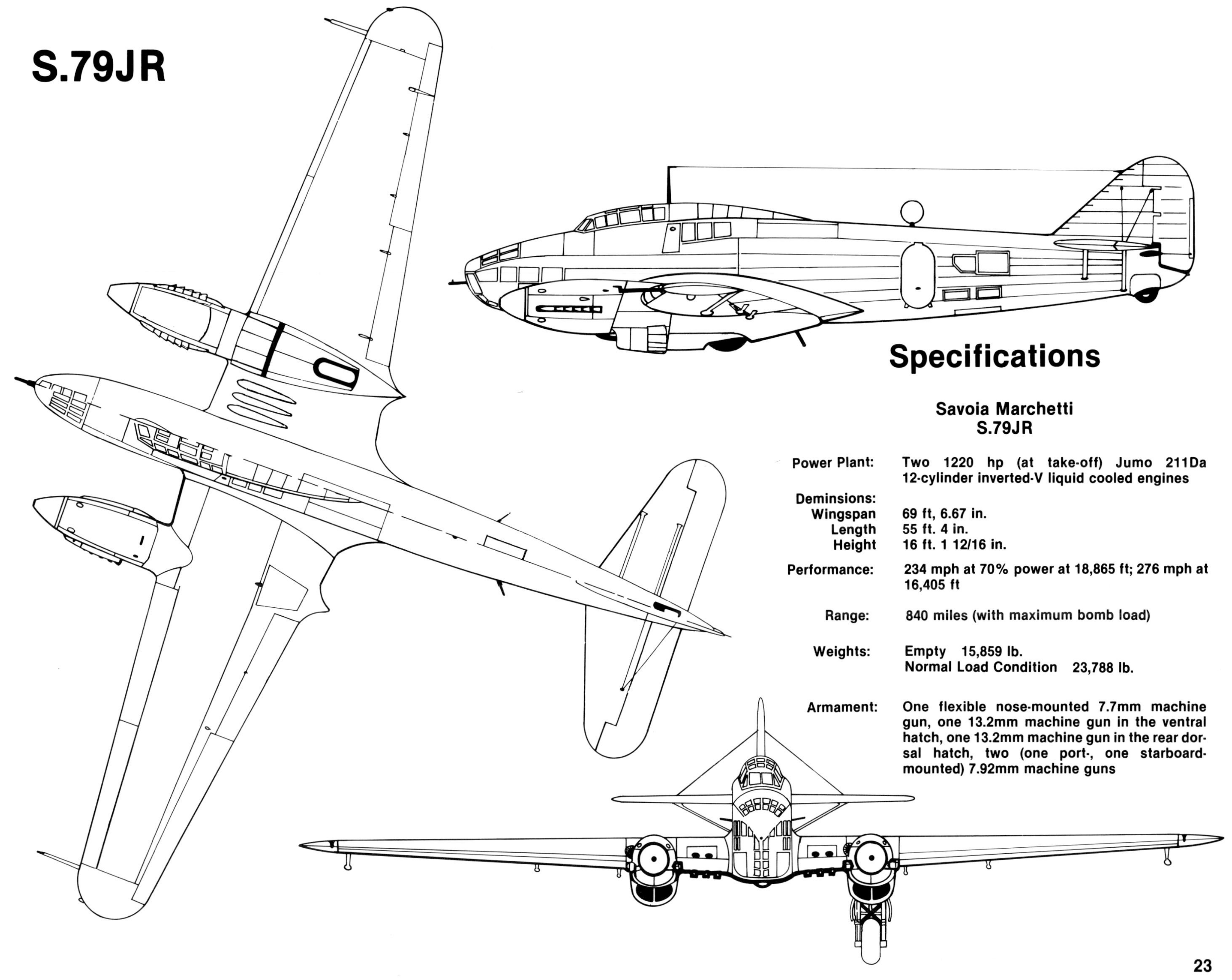

## Specifications

**Savoia Marchetti**
**S.79JR**

| | |
|---|---|
| **Power Plant:** | Two 1220 hp (at take-off) Jumo 211Da 12-cylinder inverted-V liquid cooled engines |
| **Deminsions:** | |
| **Wingspan** | 69 ft, 6.67 in. |
| **Length** | 55 ft. 4 in. |
| **Height** | 16 ft. 1 12/16 in. |
| **Performance:** | 234 mph at 70% power at 18,865 ft; 276 mph at 16,405 ft |
| **Range:** | 840 miles (with maximum bomb load) |
| **Weights:** | Empty 15,859 lb.<br>Normal Load Condition 23,788 lb. |
| **Armament:** | One flexible nose-mounted 7.7mm machine gun, one 13.2mm machine gun in the ventral hatch, one 13.2mm machine gun in the rear dorsal hatch, two (one port-, one starboard-mounted) 7.92mm machine guns |

# S.79 P.XI

The fifty-seventh S.79 airframe built by SIAI Marchetti was fitted with a trio of Piaggio P.XI RC 40 fourteen cylinder double row radial engines, an Italian development of the French Gnome & Rhone 14 Krs engine. The Piaggio powered S.79 (contrary to a widespread myth created by a wartime Italian recognition booklet) never went into production. The single example built (serialed M.M.21137) flew for first time on 24 May 1937. On 8 July 1937, with specially tuned engines, the S.79 P.XI, piloted by Biseo and Bruno Mussolini set a world's record over a 1,000 km (620 mls) course carrying a payload of 2,000 kg (4,409 lb) at a speed of 423 km/h (262.8 mph). The former record had been set by the S.79 prototype two years before.

All through the Winter of 1937 this aircraft was used for a series of record flights over 1,000 and 2,000 km (621 and 1243 mile) courses carrying payloads up to 5,000 kg (11,022 lb), flown alternatively by military pilots Biseo, Mussolini, Lucchini, Tivegna and by SIAI test pilots Bacula and De Ambrosis. On 24 February 1938 a speed record of 448 km/h (278.3 mph) was set. The final exploit of this 'special assignments' S.79 was on 4 December 1938, when the military team of Tondi and Pontonutti took the highly tuned aircraft with a load of 2,000 kg over a circuit of 2,000 km. The new record was set at 469 km/h (291.3 mph), and also setting a record for the 1,000 km. Remarkably, the publicity photos of the Italian Air Force showed a payload not of sandbags but of real bombs. The Piaggio powered S.79 was then converted into a standard bomber.

Another 'one-of' aircraft was airframe c/n 14 (serialled both M.M.20674 and M.M.21075), powered by three French Gnome & Rhone K.14 engines, the combination originally proposed for the S.79 K. This aircraft first flew on 4 March 1937 and was tested at Guidonia alongside the S.79 with Piaggio P.XI engines.

**(Above) The Piaggio P.XI powered S.79 (M.M.21137) in front of a hangar at the Guidonia test center. In the background are two SIAI S.81 bombers, the one on the left with Alfa Romeo 125 engines, the one on the right with Gnome & Rhone K.14 engines.**

**(Above) M.M.21137 at Guidonia. It has all the installations of a standard bomber, and aerodynamically appears to be particularly well finished, the tail bracing cables are faired.**

**(Below Right) The S.79 P.XI at Guidonia on 21 November 1937, when Biseo and Mussolini set a record for speed-with-payload over a 1,000 km run that was bettered nine days later by Lucchini and Tivegna in the same airplane. The forward firing machinegun has been omitted. (SMA)**

**(Below) The S.79 P.XI in 1938 with the ventral fairing eliminated to improve its performance. The propellers are variable-pitch Piaggios. Contrary to a widespread belief, the so-called S.79-II with Piaggio engines was never operational.**

S.79, 111° Stormo in Spain during 1938, carries an 'M' for Mussolini on the tail and "Fregatene" (don't give a damn!), a fascist motto, on the Black fuselage circle.

S.79 of 11ª Squadriglia, 26° Gruppo, 9° Stormo with white underwing markings for air-sea maneuvers over Sicily during the Summer of 1939.

S.79 of 253ª Squadriglia, 104° Gruppo, 46° Stormo, based at Pisa during the summer of 1940. Scheme is Sand, Green and Brown striations.

S.79 of 193ª Squadriglia, 87° Gruppo, 30° Stormo at Sciacca, Sicily during early 1941 carrying the unit's 'Electric Man' insignia.

S.79 of 58ª Squadriglia, 32° Gruppo, 10° Stormo in Sicily during 1942. 'Setti vedo ti frego' is carried on the Squadriglia insignia.

S.79 Torpedo bomber, 278ª Squadriglia, Pantelleria Island during the late spring of 1941 carrying Yellow identification cowls.

S.79 Torpedo bomber, of 256ª Squadriglia, 108° Gruppo, Berbini, Sicily during the Spring of 1943. The White fuselage band has been over sprayed with Gray for night operations

S.79 Torpedo bomber with Alfa 128 engines, of 253ª Squadriglia, 104° Gruppo, at Rhodes during the spring of 1943.

S.M.79 bis Torpedo bomber of 204ª Squadriglia, Raggruppamento Aerosiluranti, during the Summer of 1943.

A Rumanian built twin engined J.R.S.79 B during operations on the Eastern Front late in the war.

# SPANISH SERVICE

When civil war broke out in Spain during July of 1936 the Fascist Government of Italy was quick to provide aid to the Nationalists led by *Generalissimo* Franco. To this end *Regia Aeronautica* organized *Aviacion del Tercio* (Air Force of the Spanish Foreign Legion), supplying S.81s and CR. 32s in August. The conflict in Spain offered an ideal opportunity to test the new SIAI bomber, and in February of 1937 three S.79s of the 12° *Stormo* were sent to San Juan, Majorca in the Balearic Islands from which they flew sorties against Republican shipping, and land targets such as the airbase at Reus and the arsenal at Cartagena. An additional eleven machines had arrived by June. The S.79 was one of the most advanced warplanes in Spanish skies, immune from interception by all Loyalist fighters except the Soviet supplied Polikarpov I-16 Rata monoplane.

During the Spring of 1937 the Italian air component was reorganized and enlarged, as *Aviacion Legionaria* (Legionary Air Force). The S.79 quickly grew in numbers and moved to the Spanish mainland, where, under the designation 29° *Gruppo* made up of *Squadriglie* 280° and 289°, they played a major role in all further Nationalist campaigns. During the Summer of 1937 30° *Gruppo*, with *Squadriglie* 281ª and 285ª was added, forming 111° *Stormo Sparvieri* (Sparrowhawks).

8° *Stormo Falchi delle Baleari* (Hawks of the Balearics) operating in the Balearic islands was the only Italian unit to be employed as a whole in Spain. Its 28° *Gruppo* deployed from Bologna in November of 1937, followed by the 27° *Gruppo* in January of 1938. The failure on the part of the Republicans to hold or to recapture Majorca was paid for dearly by the Republicans. Right to the end of the war, the *Falchi delle Baleari* harassed government shipping, bombed its harbors along the Mediterranean coast, attacked targets in the big cities of Valencia and Barcelona, and generally applied pressure on the Republicans that was as much political as military. By the end of the war 8° *Stormo* had dropped 1,293 tons of bombs in 7,527 hours of combat flying.

On 1 January 1938, *Generale* Valle, *Regia Aeronautica* Chief of Staff, flew a secret mission from Guidonia to Barcelona, testing the S.79's adaptability to night bombing. After a successful, if risky flight (more so for a 51 year old pilot) of five and a half hours over the sea 800 kg of bombs were dropped on the Barcelona harbor.

The Nationalists were so impressed with the S.79 bomber that they used their hard won funds to order twenty-six at a cost of *Lire* 1,109,600 each, with the first aircraft being delivered in August of 1937. The first Spanish unit to begin equipping with the S.79 was *Grupo 3-G-28* taking delivery of eight S.79s (serialed 28-30 to 28-37), followed at the end of the year by *4-G-28* and *5-G-28* being equipped with S.79s (serialed 28-38 through 28-55), and finally during the Spring of 1938 *Grupo 6-G-28* was formed with eight S.79s (serialed 28-56 to 28-63).

The total number of S.79s sent to Spain was ninety-nine. At the war's end the sixty-one surviving Italian S.79s were turned over to the Spanish Air Force, receiving serials 28-64 through 28-124. Italian proposals to have the S.79 license built in Spain were not successful, but the *Jorobado* (Hunchback) as it was called by the Spanish, remained in Nationalist service during World War Two and after, with examples remaining operational in Spain and the African colonies of Ifni and Rio de Oro into the early Sixties.

The success of the S.79 in Spain, after a short initial period of secrecy, became the object of an enthusiastic propaganda campaign. Unfortunately this proved to be misleading to the *Regia Aeronautica*, which began believing its own propaganda.

**(Above) The three 'Green mice' can be seen above a White lightning bolt on the side this S.79 belonging to the 12° Stormo in the skies over Spain in 1937. It carries no lateral armament, its high speed being a sufficient defense from enemy fighters. (SMA)**

**(Below) S.79s of 111° Stormo fly low over a Spanish town. 28-11 in the center is a first series machine with the teardrop hump fairings. The engine cowlings, with a different mottle scheme, have been cannibalized from another aircraft.**

(Above) S.79s of the 111° Stormo dropping bombs over central Spain. The airplane in the foreground, from the first series, has a further set of sliding panels above the teardrop fairing. The bomb aimer is at his station, and the leg fairing 'trousers' are extended.

## Crew Entry Ladder/Door

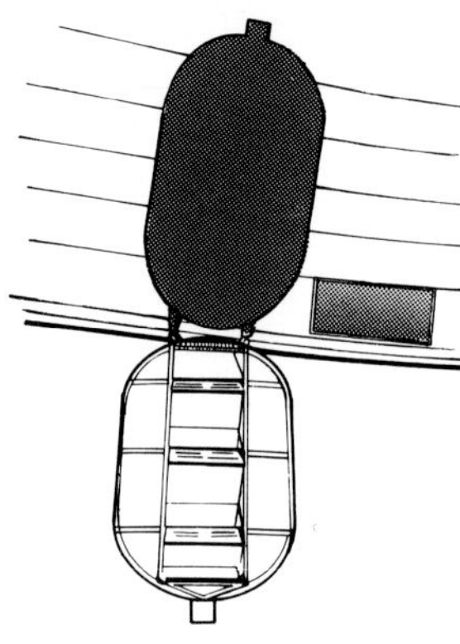

(Below) A pair of S.79s of 111° Stormo with totally different camouflage schemes, carrying the White wingtip markings of Spanish Nationalist aircraft. The good luck charm of a boy thumbing his nose, originally very small, has been painted across the fin, but couldn't take away the jinx of 28-16 adding up to seventeen (an unlucky number in Italy). In 1939 it was hit by AA and force landed with a dead pilot.

(Above) An unusual camouflage scheme and an unusual representation of the 'Green mice' in a rather modern style is carried on this first series S.79 in Spain. (Emiliani)

(Above) An unusual camouflage, believed to be Medium Green on Sand is carried on 28-2 in Spain. The Black capital M on the fin, the first letter of Mussolini's famous signature, was used as an insignia in Spain at different times by several Italian units.

(Above) 'Green Mice' S.79 in flight above the rugged dry hills of Central Spain. Gunners manning the lateral Lewis gun are watchful of enemy interceptors.

(Below) S.79s from the 10ª Squadriglia, 8º Stormo come in to land at Majorca. They fly over British, French, German and Italian warships of the Non-Intervention Committee, preforming the farcical duty of preventing European nations from sending weapons to Spain.

(Above) A Harlequin camouflage (its colors are beyond the possibility of determining) is carried on 28-26. Holes from enemy bullets are covered with Red and Yellow patches and displayed as signs of honor.

(Above) This formation of S.79s, carrying Yellow numbers are from the 8° Stormo 'Falchi delle Baleari', Spring 1938. Different colors of individual aircraft numbers identified the squadriglie within the stormo.

(Above) This surviving Spanish S.79 was converted into a VIP transport by AISA of Madrid in 1943. (AISA)

(Below) C/n 52, a former S.79 CS, became airliner I-ALAN of Ala Littoria and was used on the south Atlantic route to Brazil in 1939. This airplane has a modified V-shaped canopy and bent exhaust pipes similar to the S.M.83 airliner. The fuselage had a fuel tank installed behind the pilot's compartment followed by a four person passenger cabin. The Atlantic Lines Division of Ala Littoria gave birth to L.A.T.I. airline in 1939.

# THE S.79 AT WAR

The S.79, equipping fourteen of Italy's twenty-three bomber *Stormi* at the outbreak of the war, was the symbol of an air force that had been much vaunted since Balbo's mass flight to America. The realities of going up against modern single engine monoplane fighters, however, proved just as sobering to the *Regia Aeronautica* as it had been to unescorted RAF Wellingtons attacking Heligoland Bight, and for unescorted *Armee de l'Air* bombers attacking Invading German columns. The S.79s from 9°, 12° and 46° *Stormi* went briefly into action against France, while those based in Sardinia attacked the Bizerte naval base. The 137 operational S.79s of the five *Stormi* in Sicily were employed from the first day of war in the 'sterilization' of Malta, however the defenses of Britain's Mediterranean outpost turned out to be very effective. Italian attacks, both day and night, wound down during the Autumn, as units were recalled from Sicily and sent to reinforce Italian air power in Libya and Albania. By December of 1940, the number of operational S.79s on Sicily was down to thirty.

In North Africa the S.79 was often wastefully used hunting British armoured cars that were being used to harass the largely static Italian infantry throughout the Western Desert. One of the most tragic results of these operations was the loss of Air Marshal Italo Balbo, Governor of Libya, who was mistakenly shot down on 28 June 1940 by Italian anti-aircraft defenses at Tobruk, while returning in his S.79 from a desert search mission. While mounting strong attacks on the British bases at Sollum, Marsa Matruk and Alexandria, the S.79 suffered heavy losses to the eight gun armament of the Hawker Hurricane. When the British Army counterattacked in December of 1940, the bomber component of the African 5th Air Force was crushed. The decimated 10° and 33° *Stormi* had to be sent back to Italy (the latter being disbanded in 1941) being replaced by the 33° Gruppo and by the 9° and 41° *Stormi*. To help stop the British advance, the 34° *Stormo* was rushed to Libya, but the combination of losses in the air and during the retreat on the ground proved unbearable.

The 9°, 15° and 41° *Stormi* were transferred back to Italy, where they converted to the Cant Z.1007 bis and the Caproni 313. The 14° *Stormo* was disbanded on the mainland, and the 34° *Stormo* ceased to exist in Libya during the Spring of 1941. After just nine months of war, the Italian bomber force in North Africa had for all practical purposes been wiped out. In late Spring of 1941 the overworked 8° *Stormo* was moved to Libya, where it operated through the rest of the year.

The main target of the S.79 was the Royal Navy operating in the Mediterranean. Massed *Stormi* from Sardinia, Sicily and Italy in close formations rained bombs on enemy warship formations during the first year of the war, suffering heavy losses and learning how difficult it is for level bombers to hit ships at sea. This was compounded by the limited striking power of Italian 250 kg bombs. In Greece the S.79 was in action with the 46° *Stormo* based at Tirana, Albania. Over the harsh Balkan terrain, the S.79 supported the hard pressed Italian troops with tactical bombings.

In April of 1941 when Italy attacked Yugoslavia they met S.79s in enemy colors. The *Jugoslovensko Kraljevsko Ratno Vazduhoplovstuo* (JKRV) the Royal Yugoslav Air Force had received forty-five S.79, diverted from *Regia Aeronautica* production lots during the Fall of 1939. When hostilities began on 5 April 1941, thirty S.79s were assigned to the 7.*bombardeski Puk* (7th Bombardment Regiment) at Preljine and Gorobilje, and fifteen to the 81.*samostalna Grupa* at Ortijes-Blagaj. Yugoslavian operations, though gallant, were limited by the immediate and effective Luftwaffe and Italian strikes on their airfields. Yugoslavian S.79s briefly carried out operations against Italian forces in Albania. Four Yugoslavian S.79s managed to escape to the Middle East, where they were taken over by the RAF and given serial numbers AX702 to AX705.

Other units that used the S.79 were the Strategic Reconnaissance squadrons, performing long-range photographic missions over British bases, and the 'Sahara' squadrons, operating from desert oasis carrying out local reconnaissance and attacks against marauding British Commando units.

**(Above) When Italy entered World War II, in June of 1940, the White Cross of Savoy replaced the Green-White-Red rudder stripes. These bombers are from the 36° Stormo from Bologna, carry the two tower emblem which was symbolic of Bologna on their tails.**

**(Below) S.79 229-3 of the 32º Stormo, Sardinia. This unit was very active in bombing missions against the Royal Navy and later converted to the S.M.84, becoming a torpedo bomber unit.**

(Above) S.79 (M.M.21154) was converted to a S.79 TP VIP transport (I-ABNE). Assigned to Amedeo Duke of Aosta, Viceroy of Ethiopia, it is seen here while passing through Castelbenito, Libya, early in 1940.

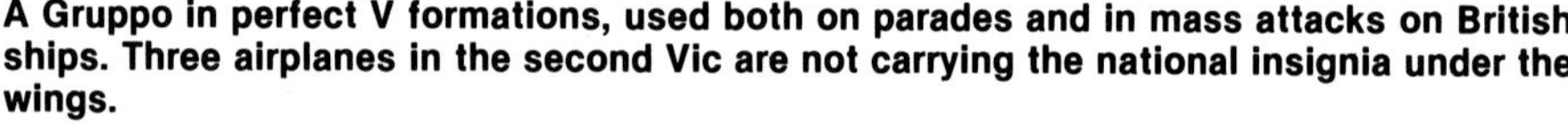

A Gruppo in perfect V formations, used both on parades and in mass attacks on British ships. Three airplanes in the second Vic are not carrying the national insignia under the wings.

(Above) S.79 54-7 of 15° Stormo, Libya, carries modified exhaust collector rings, with a line of holes on the front, probably for increased cooling.

(Below) This S.79 of 11° Stormo returns to Sicily pretty well shot up after an attack on Malta. The bomb aimer was killed in his battle position.

(Above) A formation of S.79s from the 20ª Squadriglia, 15° Stormo, in action over Libya during the Summer of 1940. White wingtips and a Black X under each wing marked Italian aircraft in North Africa during 1940.

(Below) Flight crewmen roll 500 kg bombs on the ground, which are pulled into the fuselage by a hand winch. The Flight Engineer controls the refuelling of his airplane with a hand pump out of fuel drums. The S.79 belongs to the 32° Stormo at Decimomannu, Sardinia. 13 September 1940.

(Above) Fiat C.R.42 fighters escort S.79s from Sicily during the bombing of La Valletta harbor on 2 November 1940.

(Below) Bombers of 60ª Squadriglia, 11° Stormo in 1940. The insignia on the fin is a sign post carrying the inscription "Mi fanno un baffo" (They are nothing to me). Many units had similar humorous insignias.

(Below) An Italian Junkers Ju 87R Stuka sits in front of 2-3 belonging to 45° Gruppo of 14° Stormo at Castelbenito, Libya, in early 1941.

(Above) A pair of S.79s from 50ª Squadriglia, 32° Stormo flying above Sardinia on 22 September 1940. 50-3 in the foreground has a rather unique dappled camouflage scheme which extends over the engine nacelles.

(Below) Macchi C.200 fighters escort a formation of S.79s crossing the coast of the Thirrenian Sea early in the war.

(Above) S.79 of 215ª Squadriglia, 34° Stormo at Catania, Sicily, during the Summer of 1940. These airplanes are on a mission without their forward firing machine guns.

(Below) A damaged S.79, 59-3 of the 33° Gruppo, 11° Stormo at Ain-el-Gazala, Libya on 13 September 1940. A large number of damaged S.79s were left behind during the retreat from Egypt because their big one-piece wing could not be transported.

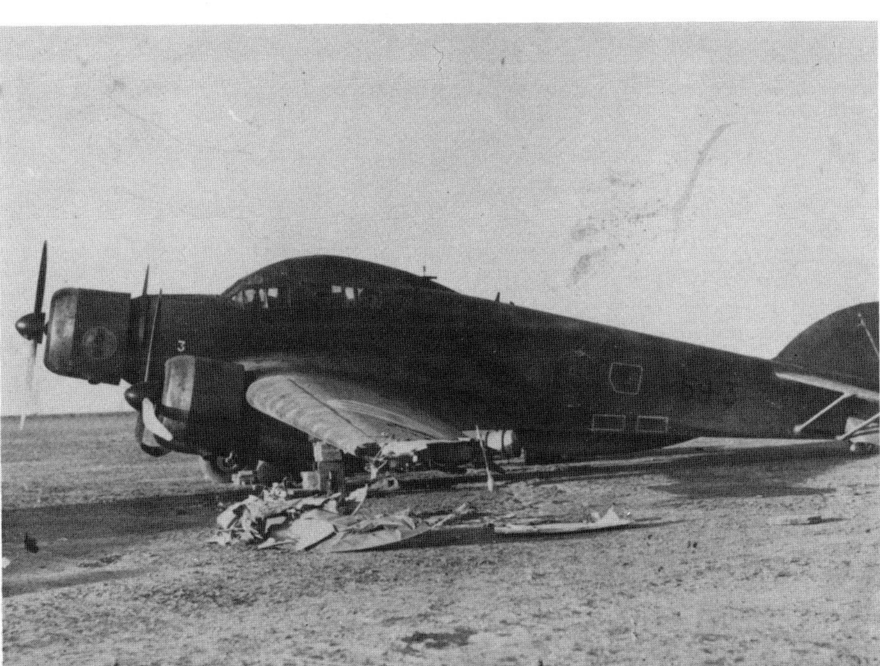

(Above) The .303 Lewis gun on a sliding mount was quickly replaced by a flexible Safat 7.7MM machine gun mounted in each window.

(Below) The hand held Safat machine gun was was belt fed from above with spent cartridges being ejected into an accordion bag below.

(Above) While 33° Gruppo was in Africa, 34° Gruppo was sent to Rhodes Island, in the Aegean Sea, with four of its airplanes experimenting with torpedo attacks. Damaged 68-3 has already been partially dismantled.

(Above) One of the few flyable S.79s captured by the RAF and SAAF in Ethiopia during the Spring of 1941 was adapted as a transport, and has had a square window added to each side.

(Below) In December of 1940 a White fuselage band was painted on all Italian airplanes, as seen on these S.79s of 30° Stormo. The third S.79, remarkably still carries the 1937 segmented Sand-Brown-Green camouflage scheme.

(Below) A Royal Yugoslav Air Force S.79. This aircraft escaped to Hungary and was returned to Italy in 1942 in exchange for two Fiat C.R.42 fighters.

(Above) 6-3, an S.79 of 44° Gruppo, captured in Ethiopia by the British. The Black X on the White band was a recognition marking adopted by Regia Aeronautica in East Africa.

(Below) A V formation of S.79s belonging to the 50ª Squadriglia, 32° Stormo, in 1941 carries another application of the popular M for Mussolini insignia.

(Above) This S.79 carries a rather over-zealous application of the White tail cross, which normally was limited to the rudder.

(Above) The 'Electrical Man' insignia of 193ª Squadriglia. The prominent White and Black wing markings have been oversprayed with Green paint. Under the cockpit in front of the generator can be seen the pennant of a Squadron commander. (Ghizzardi)

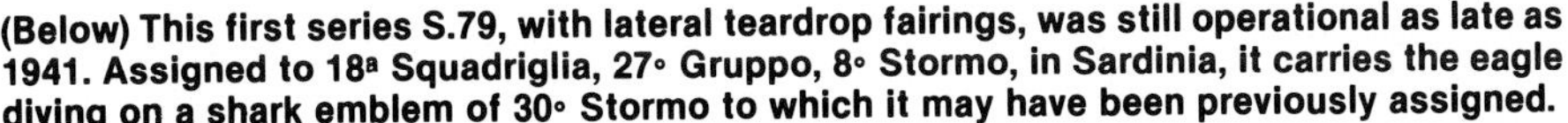

(Below) This first series S.79, with lateral teardrop fairings, was still operational as late as 1941. Assigned to 18ª Squadriglia, 27° Gruppo, 8° Stormo, in Sardinia, it carries the eagle diving on a shark emblem of 30° Stormo to which it may have been previously assigned.

# THE TORPEDO BOMBER S.79

Although *Regia Aeronautica* had operated torpedo bombers as early as World War I, there were no specialized units nor even adequate torpedoes available when World War II broke out. The S.79 had been tested with torpedoes in 1938, and in November of 1939 the new *Regia Aeronautica* Chief of Staff, *Generale* Pricolo ordered a batch of air-droppable torpedoes. The first unit, *Reparto Sperimentale Aerosiluranti* (Experimental Torpedo Bomber Unit) was formed and rushed into action with five aircraft in August of 1940. Operating from Libya, its first sortie was a night attack on Alexandria harbor on 15 August 1940, and two weeks later the four remaining aircraft made their first attack on moving ships.

On 9 September 1940 *Reparto Sperimentale Aerosiluranti* was renamed 278ª *Squadriglia, 'Quattro Gatti'* ('The Four Cats', Italian slang for very few people), which would become the nucleus of a powerful new force. The S.79 carried the 860 kg torpedo slung under the port side of the fuselage, and was initially dropped by sight, later a special viewfinder was introduced. The crew was increased by the addition of a naval officer, acting as observer and ship spotter, positioned rather precariously between the flight engineer and wireless operator.

The frantic activity of the *Quattro Gatti* paid rich dividends. On 17 September 1940 the cruiser Kent was hit by Buscaglia and Robone, and on 10 October Erasi hit the cruiser Liverpool; both ships remained out of commission for a year. On 3 December 1940 Erasi and Buscaglia struck the cruiser Glasgow. By the end of 1940, the *Squadriglia* had flown 238 sorties, carrying out 113 torpedo attacks.

With the S.79 torpedo bomber *Regia Aeronautica* had developed an excellent weapon, and quickly began to exploit it. In November of 1940 the I *Nucleo Addestramento Siluranti* (Torpedo Training Unit) was formed in Gorizia, followed by 2 *Nucleo Addestramento Siluranti* in Naples and, in 1942 3 *Nucleo Addestramento Siluranti* was formed in Pisa. From these training units, new *Squadriglie Aerosiluranti* were created, the 279ª *Squadriglia* in January of 1941, operating from Sicily, the 280ª *Squadriglia* in February, operating from Sardinia. The 281ª *Squadriglia* was formed in March of 1941 and led by the ace Carlo Emapuele Buscaglia and based in the Aegean Sea at Rhodes.

In July of 1941 283ª *Squadriglia* was formed and joined with 280ª *Squadriglia* to form 130° *Gruppo*, the first torpedo group. Other units, such as the 41° *Gruppo*, formerly of the 12° *Stormo*, and the 36° *Stormo* also were pressed into the torpedo attack role, flying the SIAI Marchetti S.M.84. However, this successor to the S.79, also a mixed construction trimotor, proved to be unreliable, mostly because of its P.XI engines. The S.M.84 was generally disliked by *Regia Aeronautica* airmen, and in 1942 the S.79 was reintroduced into those units. Paradoxically, the old, but trusted S.79 succeeded its own successor.

During 1941 the S.79 operated against British shipping with considerable success. Particularly important were the actions against the *Substance* and *Halberd* convoys supplying Malta. On 23 July 1941, *Squadriglie* 280ª and 283ª hit the cruiser Manchester and sank the destroyer Fearless. On 27 September 1941, most of the 36° *Stormo* was shot down, but a hit was scored on the battleship Nelson. S.79 torpedo pilots became the best known Italian airmen, representing what fighter aces were in other countries.

In 1942 the whole of 46° *Stormo* became a torpedo unit, while new *aerosiluranti Gruppi* were formed; 131° *Gruppo* with *Squadriglie* 279ª and 284ª in Africa, and 132° with Squadriglia 278ª and 281ª in Sicily. *Gruppo* 133° made up of reconnaissance *Squadriglie* 174ª and 175ª was directly formed in Libya, without prior training. The peak of the torpedo bomber action came with the 'Battle of mid-June' (13 to 15 June 1942) and the 'Battle of mid-August' (11 to 14 August 1942), known as OPERATIONS HARPOON and PEDESTAL to the Royal Navy, respectively. At the pinnacle of Axis success, when Rommel was marching on Alexandria, the British made an all-out effort to supply Malta under the code name HARPOON. The attacking S.79s scored hits on several freighters, again hit the unlucky cruiser Liverpool, and sank a destroyer. Against PEDESTAL, both *Regia*

**(Below) With torpedoes slung under their bellies, S.79s of 281ª Squadriglia, 132° Gruppo,prepare to fly into action against the Royal Navy attempting to re-supply Malta. (SMA)**

*Aeronautica* and the Luftwaffe engaged in one of the fiercest battles of the war, inflicting heavy losses on the British. Casualties were high, however, with the *Regia Aeronautica* losing fifty aircraft and 176 airmen, including many expert S.79 crews.

With the allied landings in French North Africa (OPERATION TORCH), 8 November 1942, the S.79 attacked ships at sea and in harbor. However, mastery of the air had fully switched to the Americans and British, and losses were very high. Even the top S.79 ace Buscaglia was shot down by Spitfires attacking Bougie. The 1941-42 average of eight torpedo hits for every aircraft lost fell to one hit for 2.5 aircraft lost during 1943. Sorties now began to be flown at night, but the efficieney of allied radars rendered even this precaution useless.

In June of 1943 most surviving S.79s were concentrated in a *Raggruppamento Aerosiluranti* based at Pisa and Siena, while only 130°, 132°, 104° *Gruppi* and 205ª and 279ª *Squadriglie* remained as independent units. The final actions took place during the invasion of Sicily, in July of 1943, with the British aircraft carrier Indomitable taking a hit off Sicily. The last S.79 *Aerosiluranti* sortie was made on the night of 8 September 1943, *after* Italy had signed the armistice with the Allies.

**(Above) Aerodynamically the single torpedo configuration was found to be far superior to the dual torpedo configuration. Few modifications had to be made in order to turn the S.79 into an excellent torpedo bomber.**

**(Below) Two torpedoes were tested under the S.79, but aircraft performance was impaired by such a load. Operationally only one torpedo was carried under the port side of the fuselage.**

**(Below) The 'Quattro Gatti' (Four Cats) that carried out the first torpedo attacks from Libyan bases in August of 1940. 278-1 armed with torpedos at El Adem airport carries White wingtips and a Black X inboard of the national roundel as required in that theater of operations. (SMA)**

# S.79 Torpedo Rack

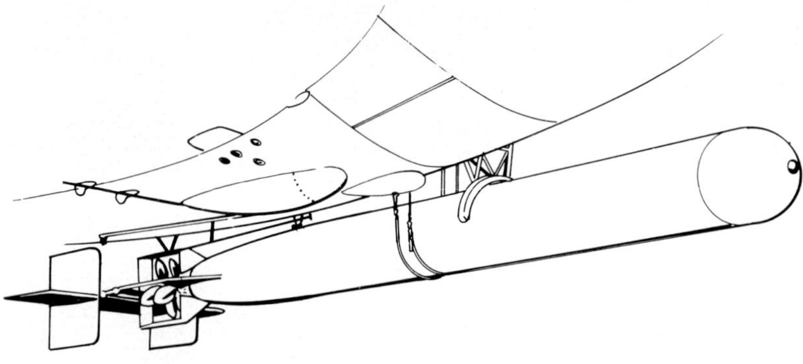

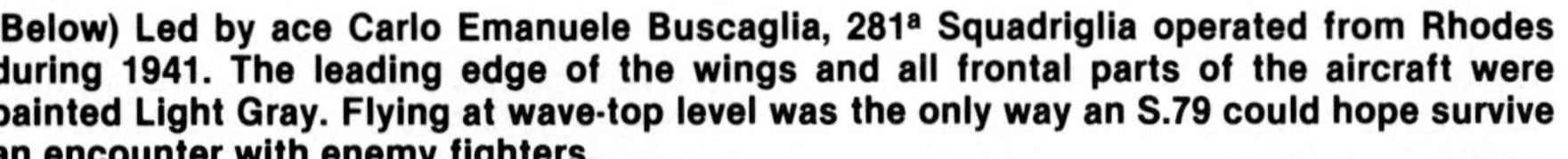

(Below) Led by ace Carlo Emanuele Buscaglia, 281ª Squadriglia operated from Rhodes during 1941. The leading edge of the wings and all frontal parts of the aircraft were painted Light Gray. Flying at wave-top level was the only way an S.79 could hope survive an encounter with enemy fighters.

(Above) S.79 torpedo bomber of 278ª Squadriglia, painted overall Dark Green, carries a 860 kg torpedo slung under its port side.

(Below) A torpedo bomber of 278ª Squadriglia in Pantelleria Island during 1941. The engine cowls carry the prescribed Yellow. A torpedo has been slung, but its aerial rudder has not been assembled yet.

(Above) This S.79 of 104° Gruppo is being loaded with a torpedo during 1942. It has the early type of exhaust stacks.

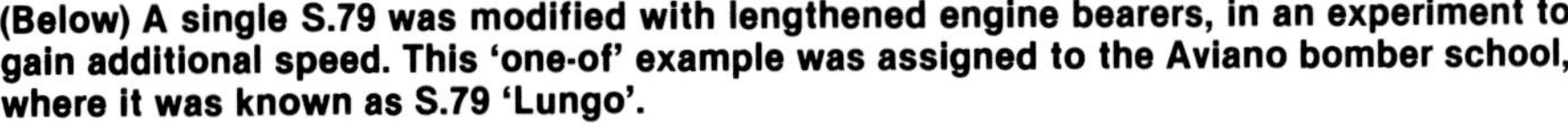

(Below) A single S.79 was modified with lengthened engine bearers, in an experiment to gain additional speed. This 'one-of' example was assigned to the Aviano bomber school, where it was known as S.79 'Lungo'.

(Above) A line-up of the 281ª Squadriglia at Gadurra, Rhodes in 1941. Half of these aircraft have had the White of their fasces insignia painted over with Light Gray camouflage and several have had the forward areas painted Light Gray.

(Below) The 132° Gruppo emblem, the Knight Orlando battling a sea monster. The motto was COL CUORE E CON L'ARMA OLTRE OGNI META (With heart and weapon, beyond every goal). (SMA)

(Above) A close formation of S.79s of the 284ª Squadriglia carry out a patrol in 1943. The fuselage band has been completely darkened, and the machine guns are equipped with flame dampers, indicating the night operations usually carried out by the torpedo bombers at this stage of the Mediterranean War.

(Above) Torpedo bombers of 283ª Squadriglia patrolling the Mediterranean between Sardinia and Tunisia, during the Spring of 1942. These S.79s are camouflaged in Light Blue-Gray, with a Light Gray fuselage identification stripe.

## Exhausts

Standard 1941 Day Exhaust

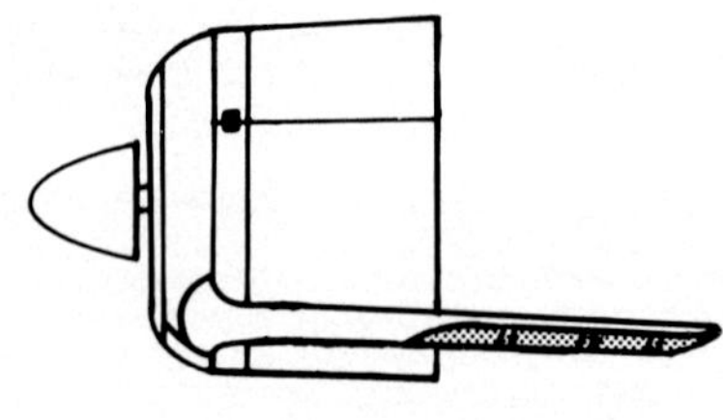

## Machine Gun

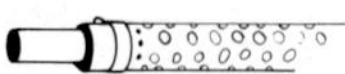

Flash Supressor

Tipo Wellington Night Exhaust

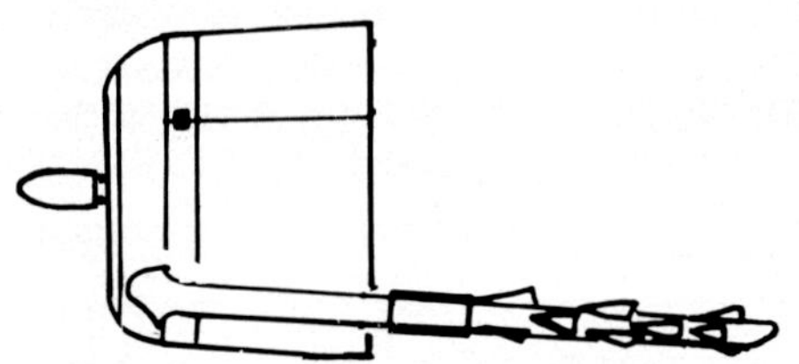

(Below) 253-10 after a forced landing on Rhodes during the Spring 1943. This is a standard S.79, with a ventral gondola, refitted with Alfa Romeo 128 engines with Alfa Romeo propellers. Camouflage is Light Gray splotches over Dark Green.

(Above) Some torpedo bombers of the 104° Gruppo carried their unit scoreboard painted on the fin. White ship profiles on 253-8 indicates that one battleship, the carrier Eagle, two cruisers and four steamers have been hit.

(Above) Three S.79s of the 253ª Squadriglia fly in formation with two German Junkers Ju 88s over Rhodes' Castle of the Knights during practice flights for coordinated dive bomber and torpedo attacks in March of 1943.

(Below) An S.79 of the 174ª Squadriglia R.S.T. swoops down to deck level to check out a steamer off the African coast. Two Strategic Reconnaissance units (174 and 175) had been joined into the 133° Gruppo Aerosiluranti during the spring of 1942 in Libya, but by the end of the year the Gruppo had been disbanded.

# S.M.79 bis

Throughout its production life few modifications were made to the S.79, none of them major. Only in 1942 did the S.79 begin receiving an ethyl injection boosted system which increased the power of the Alfa Romeo 126 powerplants from 680 hp to 900 hp for up to twenty minutes. As more and more missions were undertaken at night, the S.79 had begun receiving flame-damping exhaust pipes and flash suppressors on the muzzles of their machine guns. Under Buscaglia's lead 132° *Gruppo* modified an S.79 by removing the ventral gondola and installed a 700 liter fuel tank in the fuselage, giving it an endurance of over ten hours. From the Spring of 1943, many S.79s had their engines replaced with Alfa Romeo 128 RC 18 engines turning constant speed Alfa Romeo propellers. The Alfa 128 was essentially similar to the Alfa 126 but developed its highest power rating of 860 HP at 1,800 meters, instead of the 3,400 meters of the 126. It was, therefore, better suited to low-flying torpedo bombers.

All these modifications were put together in a single variant under the designation S.M.79 bis. By May of 1943 ten S.79 bis torpedo bombers were delivered by refurbishing and updating older airframes. The S.M.79 bis had an additional fuselage fuel tank providing it with a total capacity of 4,750 liters of fuel, instead of the 3,320 liters of the earlier S.79. Another important modification was the adoption of a repeating compass, which allowed the use of a torpedo with a magnetic fuse. These upgraded S.79 torpedo bombers were prepared for *OPERAZIONE SCOGLIO* (OPERATION ROCK), an attack on Gibraltar.

Starting from Istres, from which the 'Green Mice' had operated some six years earlier, the best *siluranti* pilots in the *Regia Aeronautica* took off in ten S.M.79 bis torpedo bombers on 19 June 1943. Only two aircraft managed to reach the enemy base and drop their torpedos, without results. Ten days later the S.M.79 bis successfully attacked the port of Oran.

**(Above) The first appearance of the S79 bis at the Guidonia test center. Armor plate has been added to the crew entry door. The night exhaust pipes were called 'Tipo Wellington' (SMA)**

After the armistice Mussolini, under *Nazi* patronage, formed the *Repubblica Sociale Italiana* (RSI) in German-controlled Northern Italy, which continued fighting against the Allies. The new *Aeronautica Nazionale Repubblicana* formed the torpedo *Gruppo Buscaglia* with S.M.79 bis rebuilt from S.79 airframes, plus a small number of new aircraft built from SIAI stored components.

The republican S.M.79 bis went into action against American ships off the Anzio beachhead on 10 and 13 March 1944. On 10 April, after another successful attack off Anzio, the unit commander, Captain Faggioni, was shot down and killed. When the RSI found that Buscaglia, presumed dead, was actually alive and flying with the Allies the unit was renamed *Gruppo Faggioni*. The new commander, Captain Marini, led twelve airplanes in an attack against Gibraltar on 4 June 1944, again taking off from Istres. Four ships were claimed sunk and two damaged. During the Summer of 1944 *Gruppo Faggioni* moved to Greece, operating over the Eastern Mediterranean. The last victory was scored on 5 January 1945, with two S.M.79 bis sinking a 5,000 ton steamer in the Adriatic Sea.

**(Below) One of the initial ten S.M.79 bis that were prepared for OPERAZIONE SCOGLIO, the attack on Gibraltar, which was carried out on 19 June 1943. Aircraft in the background are German DFS 230 and Gotha Go 242 assault gliders.**

(Above) Some of the most famous aerosiluranti pilots just before the 19 June attack on Gibraltar. From the left, Graziani, Di Bella, Mellei, Marini and Cimicchi. Graziani, Di Bella and Cimicchi were awarded the Gold Medal, Italy's highest award; they all survived the war. (SMA)

(Above) The S.79 was used as a flying test-bed for the Isotta Fraschini Zeta engine at the Reggiane factory, Reggio Emilia. The Zeta, a twenty-four cylinder X-shaped engine, was planned for use on the Reggiane Re.2004 fighter. Both Reggiane and Isotta Fraschini belonged to the Caproni group. (Emiliani)

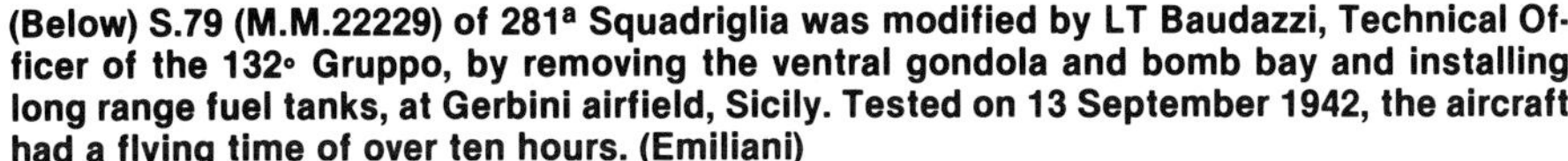

(Below) S.79 (M.M.22229) of 281ª Squadriglia was modified by LT Baudazzi, Technical Officer of the 132° Gruppo, by removing the ventral gondola and bomb bay and installing long range fuel tanks, at Gerbini airfield, Sicily. Tested on 13 September 1942, the aircraft had a flying time of over ten hours. (Emiliani)

(Above) Airmen of the Republican National Air Force celebrate Mass and swear allegiance to their battle flag in front of their S.79s. New aircraft markings included the Italian flag on the fuselage and fin, and two inverted Black fasces surrounded by a Black square on the upper and lower wing surfaces.

(Right) The torpedo on this republican S.M.79 bis has been graced with a devil's face painted on its warhead.

(Below) B1-3, indicating third airplane of the first squadron of Gruppo Buscaglia. Carrying the postage stamp markings of the Aeronautica Nazionale Repubblicana, is a rather war-weary looking S.79. The White cross of the Regia Aeronautica on the rudder has been rather ineffectively painted over. (SMA)

(Right) Most S.M.79 bis aircraft featured improved defensive armament, with lateral 12.7MM guns firing from armored windows aft of the crew entry door replacing the open window positions of the S.79.

## Lateral Armament

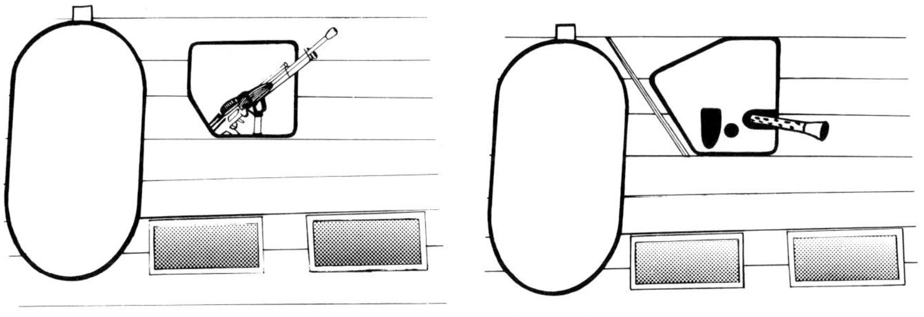

(Below Right) The flamedampened and lengthened central exhaust pipes installed for night operations caused troubles by overheating the underslung torpedo.

(Below) There has been no evidence that the S.79 bis was armed with a 20MM cannon except for a single experimental example belonging to the Gruppo Buscaglia.

(Above) S.79 102-6 of the Co-belligerent Regia Aeronautica in Southern Italy, 1945. This airplane is painted overall Dark Green. The ventral gondola has been removed and the air vent behind the hump indicates a fuselage tank has been installed. The engines are Alfa 126s.

(Below) An S.M.79 bis adapted as a transport, during the immediate post-war years carrying the Red-White-Green roundels re-introduced by the Regia Aeronautica and the present Aeronautica Militare. The aircraft is serialled M.M.253??, indicating that it belonged to the final series of S.79s (M.M.25366-25395) built by Reggiane during the Spring of 1943.

## S.79 Transport

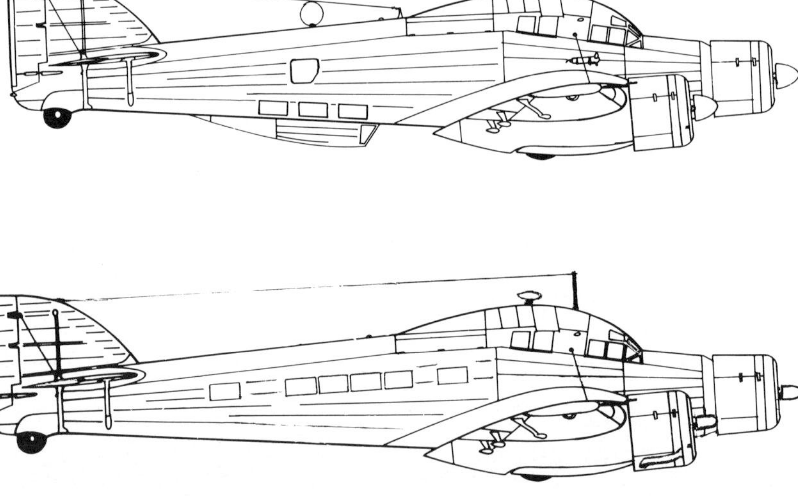

# S.79 TRANSPORT

As early as 1939 several S.79 had been converted to *Trasporto Personalita* (personnel transports) and assigned to high commanders. Their bomb bay was replaced by a passenger cabin, and windows were added to the fuselage sides. Fast and reliable, the S.79 performed extremely well in the job for which it had originally been designed, carrying seven or eight people over medium distances at high speed.

After the Armistice in September of 1943, *Regia Aeronautica* collected all possible aircraft in Allied-occupied Southern Italy, and from 13 October 1943 began operations against Germany as the Co-belligerent Air Force. Twenty-nine S.79s were gathered by the Co-belligerents in the South and operated by 3° *Stormo Trasporti* consisting of 2° *Gruppo* (102ª and 103ª *Squadriglie*), and 98° *Gruppo* (240ª and 241ª *Squadriglie*) dropping leaflets over Northern Italy and as fast liaison aircraft. The S.79's service included secret missions with OSS agents. After VE Day the S.79 was operated by the *Corrieri Aerei Militari* (Military Air Couriers) ferrying government personalities and selected passengers over a country that had had most of its rail and road system destroyed. The S.79 flew alongside S.M.82 transports and converted Martin Baltimore bombers.

During the post-war years the S.79 survived as a target-towing aircraft and transport, and was finally replaced by the Beechcraft C-45. As late as 1960 the dump heaps of Italy were still full of S.79 hulks. However, a few years later, the only example of an S.79 available for exhibition in the Italian Air Force Museum had to be donated by Lebanon. Lebanon had received four S.79s, some of which were eleven years old, in 1949 using them as fast couriers with serials L-110 to L-113.

**(Above) Memories of wings past. A Caproni 100, with stunt pilot Magrini at the controls, flies above an S.M.79 bis of 3a ZAT (3rd Air Region). In the background are Beechcraft C-45's with the markings of Pisa's 46ª Aerobrigate, descendant of the 46° Stormo that fought all over The Mediterranean while flying the S.79.**

**(Below) L-112, one of four S.M.79s delivered to Lebanon in 1949, was returned to Italy where it was exhibited in Turin during the early Seventies. In its present location, Vigna di Valle Air Museum, it carries a wartime camouflage.**

SS1036 F6F Hellcat in Action

SS1045 P-51 Mustang in Action

SS1044 Messerschmitt Bf109 in Action Part 1
SS1057 Messerschmitt Bf109 in Action Part 2

SS1039 Spitfire in Action

# THE MAGNIFICENT SEVEN!

ONLY $5.95 EACH

SS1067 P-47 Thunderbolt in Action

SS1029 F4U Corsair in Action

SS1059 A6M Zero in Action